LOOSE PARTS 4

Other Redleaf Press books by Lisa Daly and Miriam Beloglovsky

Loose Parts: Inspiring Play in Young Children

Loose Parts 2: Inspiring Play with Infants and Toddlers

Loose Parts 3: Inspiring Culturally Sustainable Environments

Early Learning Theories Made Visible

Loose Parts 4

INSPIRING 21ST-CENTURY LEARNING

Lisa Daly and Miriam Beloglovsky ■ Photography by Jenna Knight

Redleaf Press®
www.redleafpress.org
800-423-8309

Published by Redleaf Press
10 Yorkton Court
St. Paul, MN 55117
www.redleafpress.org

First edition 2019
Senior editor: Heidi Hogg
Managing editor: Douglas Schmitz
Cover design: Renee Hammes
Cover and interior photographs: Jenna Knight
Interior design: Erin Kirk New
Typeset in Berkeley Oldstyle Book
Printed in the United States of America
26 25 24 23 22 21 20 19   1 2 3 4 5 6 7 8

Library of Congress Cataloging-in-Publication Data

Names: Daly, Lisa, author. | Beloglovsky, Miriam, author. | Knight, Jenna, photographer.
Title: Loose parts 4 : inspiring 21st-century learning / Lisa Daly and Miriam Beloglovsky ; Photography by Jenna Knight.
Other titles: Loose parts four
Description: First edition. | Saint Paul, MN : Redleaf Press, [2020] | Includes bibliographical references and index. | Summary: "In the newest installment of the popular, award-winning Loose Parts series, Lisa Daly and Miriam Beloglovsky focus on family engagement and competency building. Lisa and Miriam explain the value of loose parts, detail how to integrate loose parts into the environment and children's play, and specifically focus on loose parts for children in family environments—helping educators engage families and extend learning beyond the classroom"— Provided by publisher.
Identifiers: LCCN 2019024276 (print) | LCCN 2019024277 (ebook) | ISBN 9781605545899 (paperback) | ISBN 9781605545905 (ebook)
Subjects: LCSH: Play. | Early childhood education—Activity programs. | Creative activities and seat work.
Classification: LCC LB1139.35.P55 D37 2020 (print) | LCC LB1139.35.P55 (ebook) | DDC 372.21—dc23
LC record available at https://lccn.loc.gov/2019024276
LC ebook record available at https://lccn.loc.gov/2019024277

Printed on acid-free paper

To all who love to play

To all who love to learn

To all who embrace change

To all who believe in a hopeful future

Contents

Acknowledgments

My hope is that with this book, we change the discourse in education from children's readiness to children's success. This hope became visible through ongoing conversations with my supportive friends. I dedicate this book equally to all of them—Michael Leeman, Annie White, Michelle Grant-Groves, Jeannette Mulhern, Tim Craig, Heidi Brahms, Chris Marks, Darcelle Lahr, Laurel Doyle, Larrisa Wilkinson—and to all of the educators who devote their time and energy to advocate for children's right to play. I am honored to be the mother of two incredible daughters who, in their own way, fight every day for equity and justice. I am also in awe of my great-niece Dominique Leibman for her willingness to speak up and stand up for what is right. She gives me hope for a future where social justice is embraced and equity exists for everyone. I want to thank the staff at Redleaf Press for their commitment to quality, which is always inspiring. **—Miriam Beloglovsky**

As with all our books, there are many people who collaborated with us from idea to reality. My special appreciation goes out to the following people who graciously allowed us to capture their children at play and opened their homes for photography: Angela and Jules, Ashley and Will, Bob and Erica, Eddie, Heidi, Jarred and Emily, Jenn and Chris, Lance, and Mary. As always, my family, friends, and colleagues have been a tremendous support throughout the writing of this book. I thank you all for your generous encouragement, reflection, and dedication. Jenna, thank you for once more capturing inspiring photographs. I want to acknowledge Miriam for her contributions to the Loose Parts series. It has been an amazing journey. To all those at Redleaf Press, thank you for your vision, support, technical expertise, and creativity. May this book inspire educators, families, and policy makers to advocate for play-based learning and make play a priority in the lives of children. **—Lisa Daly**

Part 1
Introduction to Loose Parts for the Twenty-First Century

The twenty-first century has brought constant change and demands for education that go beyond academic readiness. Through a play-based approach with loose parts, children will cultivate the knowledge, capacities, and dispositions to thrive as adults in a global society and face the challenges of an unknown future.

Every new generation of children faces a future world that we can't yet imagine. Children born today may not experience using paper currency, hardcover books, or cursive handwriting, or learning how to drive a car. Our society and technology are advancing at such a rapid pace that imagining what's on the horizon for our children's future is difficult. Upon adulthood every generation encounters changes in life that bring joy but also often come with criticism, uncertainty, rejection, and failure. How you tackle these obstacles will determine how you succeed in life. A major goal of both teaching and parenting is to prepare children for life, but what really matters?

One may believe that achievement and happiness are critical to being successful in the future, but who defines success? Success is often defined in terms of wealth or fame, but this definition seems rather narrow. For many individuals, obtaining a medical degree or becoming a professional athlete are signs of achievement, but aren't there unhappy doctors and athletes in the world? An early childhood educator may be fulfilled working with young children, but if prosperity is defined as financial gain, the low wages of an educator do not qualify as affluence. Looking at our educational system, we can clearly see that we value skill building for our children; after all, they need to be prepared to enter the workforce with marketable skills. But is this enough to be successful?

What children need more than skills and success is to build capacities. Skills are abilities, either physical or mental, that are inherent or acquired. Capacities, on the other hand, involve the *potential* to develop skills and the power to learn. Capacity building involves strengthening an individual's ability to hold, receive, or absorb. Everyone has the potential to build capacities. Capacity allows you to grasp change effectively, which is important for handling unforeseen possibilities. Young children can be properly prepared for the future by developing their full capacities for creativity, critical thinking, and active engagement in the world. Through open-ended play, children develop capacities for imagination, compassion, empathy, learning, resourcefulness, respect, initiative, vision, and sustained purpose, and for examining problems, and constructing solutions. Our goal as educators and as parents is to help all the children in our lives learn who they are so that they may go forward into adulthood with the confidence that they are equipped to thrive.

CHAPTER 1

Twenty-First-Century Skills That Matter

Children need the social, emotional, and cognitive capacities that are going to get them into the twenty-first century as thriving adults and effective citizens. In a world where what we know is changing so swiftly, children need the knowledge, abilities, character traits, and work behaviors that are essential for navigating the future. These are called twenty-first-century skills. Multiple educational frameworks have been developed that integrate twenty-first-century skills into key subjects such as English, mathematics, arts, science, and history for high school and college students.

Life Skills

The New World of Work presents the top twenty-first-century skills for developing curriculum to prepare community college students with the competencies, attributes, and traits that are highly valued by employers and important to academic success (Schulz and Gill 2014). Their Top 10 Skills include adaptability, analysis/solution mind-set, collaboration, communication, digital fluency, entrepreneurial mind-set, empathy, resilience, self-awareness, and social/diversity awareness. According to the Centre for Educational Research and Innovation (CERI), the capacity for lifelong learning is more essential than memorizing facts and procedures for future success (OECD and CERI 2008). Research from educational professionals also reveals the skills, knowledge, and expertise students must master to succeed in work and life. Ellen Galinsky (2010), author of *Mind in the Making: The Seven Essential Life Skills Every Child Needs*, asserts that children absolutely need to learn concepts and facts, but equally important are life skills. What are the life skills that experts believe children need to be successful in the future?

Knowingness

To succeed in the twenty-first century, children will need to accurately assess their personalities, strengths, and areas of growth and seek ways to continually develop skills. Life will always have setbacks, so resilience and learning from mistakes is important. Developing an awareness of how to positively adapt to change and how to be flexible is beneficial. The more you know about yourself, the better you are at adapting to life changes. Knowingness includes these skills:

- self-awareness
- critical reflection
- identity and learning to be
- adaptability and resilience

Connections

When children grow into adulthood, the world in which they find themselves will involve the capacities of connection, communication, and collaboration. When we experience loving connections, we feel supported and valued. Good communication is central to strong, healthy relationships and maintaining satisfying personal interactions. Adults need to be able to communicate effectively through writing, speech, and multimedia formats such as visual imagery. Collaboration is necessary to work competently and cooperatively with local and global coworkers to solve problems, complete projects, and create innovative ideas. Connections include the following:

- a sense of belonging
- children as skillful communicators
- building empathy
- collaboration and moral development

Engagement

In the workforce and in our home lives, adults need to work independently and complete tasks without direct supervision. We need initiative and self-direction to use time productively, manage workload efficiently, and persevere when we may not necessarily feel like it. We are more content when absorbed with meaningful work. Attributes of engagement include being passionate, committed, and invested in what you do. Engagement involves these areas:

- focus and concentration
- children as scientists
- productive agency
- the power of solitude

Risk

Thriving in a new global economy requires the ability to take risks. People who push boundaries and break the ordinary mind-set by using materials and visualizing ideas differently are risk-takers. Risk-taking is a critical trait of creativity.

Children need to experience risk physically, socially, and intellectually if they are to advance their skills and learn how to keep themselves safe. Life involves risks in all areas. It requires risk to master physical challenges such as learning to walk or ride a bicycle, to master a social challenge such as initiating a conversation with an unknown person, or to master an intellectual challenge such as learning to read or discovering a solution to a problem. Children must experience and conquer challenges to learn how to navigate daily life experiences when they are older. Risk includes the following:

- learning about risk-taking capacities
- physical risks
- social-emotional risks
- intellectual risks

Innovative Thinking

The capacity to think analytically involves our competence with understanding, applying, analyzing, evaluating, and creating. These verbs, identified in Bloom's taxonomy, help us describe and classify observable knowledge, skills, attitudes, behaviors, and beliefs (Yale Poorvu Center for Teaching and Learning 2018). Each verb reflects a more advanced way of thinking, which is an indication of cognitive activity. Inquiry thinking is important, as using higher-end thinking skills helps us research and evaluate information effectively and proficiently. Innovative thinking comprises these areas:

- the cycle of innovation
- design thinking
- inquisitiveness and curiosity
- uncertainty and ambiguity

Creativity

Characteristics of creative thinkers include being open-minded, original, imaginative, communicative, and flexible. To equip ourselves for the world's rapid transformation, we need to be able to look at and solve problems from different perspectives. Such outside-the-box thinking helps us respond to challenges and develop unique and useful solutions. Creativity is fostered as children play with materials that lend themselves to various uses. As children engage with open-ended materials, they discover alternatives, find solutions, create something new, or combine materials in novel but meaningful ways. Creativity includes these areas:

- messiness
- humor and joy
- curiosity and play
- intellectual and affective engagement

Leadership

Advances in technology during the twenty-first century have resulted in teams of individuals with diverse socioeconomic, generational, cultural, and national backgrounds working on common projects. Becoming aware of one's own perspectives and cognizant of other cultural perspectives is vital to building a foundation of informed cross-cultural communication, that is, how people from differing backgrounds effectively communicate. Additionally citizens in the twenty-first century should have capacities to promote social justice, altruism, and sustainability. Our world needs individuals who advocate for equal economic, political, and social rights; serve others; and support, uphold, or strengthen resources, values, culture, and traditions to ensure continuation for future generations. Leadership includes these subjects:

- open-mindedness and perspective-taking
- altruism and social justice
- building sustainability
- a global perspective

Digital Fluency

One twenty-first-century skill that will not be explored in this text is digital or technical fluency, which is the ability to effectively and proficiently navigate and function in the digital world. We recognize the importance of digital fluency for understanding, selecting, and using technologies and technological systems, but we believe that technology should be introduced at an appropriate developmental age and not according to capability. Just because a child has the ability to use technology does not necessarily mean that they should.

Young children are motivated to be mentally active in the context of physical activity (DeVries and Zan 2012). This means that children learn best through movement and dynamic investigation. A child's instinctive and inquisitive desire to actively engage with their environment may be suppressed when introduced to technology at too early of an age. You may be surprised to learn that many parents who live or work in the tech world of Silicon Valley, home to many of the world's largest tech corporations, limit or ban their own children's use of technology (Weller 2018). These parents have major concerns about technology's influence on their children's emotional and social development.

The American Academy of Pediatrics (2016) addresses the influence of media on the health and development of children from birth to five years of age. Their recommendation is to avoid digital media for children younger than eighteen to twenty-four months and limit screen use for children two to five years of age to one hour per day of high-quality programming that you watch with your child. Remember that the early years are a time of critical brain development, building secure relationships, and establishing healthy behaviors.

Healthy play experiences form the foundation for brain development and lay the groundwork for all future relationships and learning. Time spent engaged in play during childhood supports learning by doing and leads to the development of physical, emotional, social, and cognitive competence. The foundation for healthy growth and development is much like the construction of a bridge. The stability of a structure is contingent on a solid foundation, and a bridge's design, materials, and construction affect the bridge's stability. So it is with children. To lay a solid foundation in childhood, you need to understand the bigger picture of experiences, skills, and capacities that are necessary for a child to grow into a thriving adult.

Play

"Play does seem to open up another part of the mind that is always there, but that, since childhood, may have become closed off and hard to reach. When we treat children's play as seriously as it deserves, we are helping them feel the joy that's to be found in the creative spirit. We're helping ourselves stay in touch with that spirit, too. It's the things we play with and the people who help us play that make a great difference in our lives" (F. Rogers 2003, 83).

Young children learn best through self-directed play. There is an abundance of evidence supporting this fact from scientists, psychologists, physicians, anthropologists, and historians. Children's lives are enriched through free play that is pleasurable, self-motivated, imaginative, spontaneous, creative, and free from specific adult-imposed goals and outcomes. The knowledge that the most important way children learn is through play is vital for families and educators. By *play* we mean child-directed experiences that are free from adult interference and micromanagement. We are concerned by adults who hover while children play or interrupt a child's play by asking test-like questions, such as "What color is that?" or "What shape is that?" It seems as if they want to seize every moment as an educational opportunity. Consider a parent at the park with their daughter who is happily creating a habitat for her plastic panda bear. The parent quizzes, "What kind of bear is that? Where does it live? What color is it? How many legs does it have?" The poor child cannot relax and simply play with her toy panda bear. Our longtime mentor Bev Bos shared the invaluable wisdom of never asking a child a question that you can answer. One time a teacher asked a three-year-old boy what color he was using. He replied, "You're my teacher, and you don't know the color blue?" Such questions are shallow and closed in nature with one correct response that restricts deeper critical thinking, and this kind of questioning interferes with play.

Throughout our years as professors of early childhood education, we have discovered that adults do not have a clear understanding of what play really is. Most adults report instances of adult- and time-dominated activities as play, when in fact such activities do not meet the criteria of play. Let's take a look at what play really is and the value of play for children.

What Is Play?

Play is compelling, powerful, and engaging, yet its complex and multifaceted nature makes it hard to easily define. In fact there is not a single agreed-upon definition of play, but there are properties of play that distinguish it from other

behaviors. Play experts include the following characteristics of play in their definitions (Herron and Sutton-Smith 1971; Brown 2009; Gray 2013):

- Play is freely chosen, a self-selected and self-directed expression of freedom. Play is doing what is desired rather than doing what is required.
- Play is intrinsically motivated, inherently engaging, satisfying, and serves as its own reward. Children play because it is gratifying in itself, not because of an external reward.
- Play is process oriented and done for its own sake. In play the focus is on doing the activity and not the end result or product.
- Play is fun, enjoyable, and engaging for the participants. Expressions of positive emotions such as smiles and laughter often accompany play.
- Play is nonliteral. In play children can suspend reality and transform objects, actions, and situations to fit their imagination. Play is pretend. The plot, setting, characters, and conflict in play can be negotiated as the play unfolds and are not bound to reality.
- Play is active. It involves dynamic interaction with objects, big ideas, and people. Our senses, physical skills, and intellectual capacities are engaged when we play.

Why Is Play Valuable?

LEARNING

Play is the process that helps assimilate all that we know, learn, understand, and feel. Early childhood expert Erica Christakis (2016a, 146) states, "Play is the fundamental building block of human cognition, emotional health, and social behavior. Play improves memory and helps children learn to do mathematical problems in their heads, take turns, regulate their impulses, and speak with greater complexity."

DEVELOPMENT

Play reflects development, reinforces development, and results in development. A child's development in the physical, social, emotional, and cognitive domains is revealed while they play. Play reinforces development as they use previously acquired competencies and capabilities to be in control, practice new skills, and use those skills creatively. Play results in development, seen in qualitative changes to their understanding, reasoning, and processing capacities.

HEALTH AND WELL-BEING

The American Academy of Pediatrics is concerned about the decline of play and recommends that all children have ample, unscheduled, and independent non–screen time to be creative, to reflect, and to decompress (Ginsburg 2007). Play is "essential to the health and well-being of children and promote[s] the development of creativity, imagination, self-confidence, self-efficacy, as well as physical, social, cognitive and emotional strength and skills" (United Nations Committee on the Rights of the Child 2013). Play is also the best method for children to learn and the best defense against the stress and pressures that society imposes on children (S. Brown 2009). Through play experiences, children gain competencies to flourish in an uncertain future.

SKILL ACQUISITION

A strong link exists between play and learning for young children. When children play, they use their abilities, knowledge, and understanding in different ways and contexts. According to psychologist and educator David Elkind (2008, 1), "Through play, children create new learning experiences, and these self-created experiences enable them to acquire social, emotional, and intellectual skills they could not acquire in any other way."

MEANING-MAKING

Through freely chosen, active, enjoyable, and engaging play, children learn concepts, test ideas, confirm theories, and develop skills. When young children engage in play experiences, they will naturally construct meaning from their world and develop inquiry skills for future learning (Pistorova and Slutsky 2017).

FULL POTENTIAL

Play during early childhood is essential if children are to reach their full potential. Enjoyable play with open-ended materials awakens potential by developing creativity and imagination and promotes joy, which is necessary for self-esteem and health. The International Play Association's (2008) Declaration of the Child's Right to Play states that "play, along with the basic needs of nutrition, health, shelter, and education, is vital to develop the potential of all children."

The Demise of Play

During the last several decades, there has been an ongoing movement to improve children's academic performance that has resulted in academics being integrated into preschool, reducing play. Young children are being asked to accomplish more and more tasks that were once reserved for kindergarten or first grade. Erika Christakis (2016b) argues that "the preoccupation with accountability has led to a set of measures that favor shallow mimicry and recall behaviors, such as learning vocabulary lists and recognizing shapes and colors . . . while devaluing complex, integrative, and syncretic learning."

In a report from the Alliance for Childhood, researchers chronicle the radical changes that have taken place in kindergarten practice over the last ten to twenty years. They describe how "children now spend far more time being instructed and tested in literacy and math than they do learning through play and exploration, exercising their bodies, and using their imaginations. . . . Many children struggle to live up to academic standards that are developmentally inappropriate" (Miller and Almon 2009, 15). Researchers, educators, and writers alike seem to agree that that the push for rigorous early education has ignored the research on how young children learn best.

For four decades, David Elkind (1988) has cautioned families, educators, and health professionals about the damaging effects of pushing children too much, too fast, and too soon and pressuring them to achieve. Children are harmed when we hurry them through childhood. Pushing children too hard is unhealthy, as it increases overwhelming stress and prohibits the natural unfolding of development. Elkind emphasizes the importance of adults who advocate for children and protect childhood from the dangerous trend toward teaching skills earlier and earlier.

In *The Hiding Place*, Corrie ten Boom recalls a story of her father protecting her from learning too much, too soon, too fast. On a train trip from Amsterdam, Corrie asked her father a difficult question that he felt she was too young to fully understand the answer. After a thoughtful pause, he asked Corrie to carry his traveling case off the train. She attempted to pick it up but said, "It's too heavy." Her father replied, "Yes, and it would be a pretty poor father who would ask his little girl to carry such a load. It's the same way, Corrie, with knowledge. Some knowledge is too heavy for children. When you are older and stronger you can bear it. For now, you must trust me to carry it for you" (ten Boom 1971, 41–42). Often young children seem very capable of carrying heavy loads in the form of knowledge, media viewing, or participation in extracurricular activities, but we need to question if they can truly handle it, for how long, and if it is indeed necessary for them to do so at this moment.

Challenges Families Face

Parenting is one of the most rewarding jobs there is, but it is not without trials. Conflicting messages, overscheduling, and limited financial resources are serious problems that families face while they nurture, protect, influence, and guide their children's physical, emotional, social, intellectual, and spiritual development. Goals of parenting may include teaching children to be independent, competent, resilient, able to solve problems, and moral. But one of the biggest tasks of parenting and society is to preserve childhood, and there is no shortage of challenges to overcome along the way.

CONFLICTING MESSAGES

Families want what is best for their children, yet they are confronted with an overabundance of advice and messages that can be confusing and overwhelming. They want their children to enter school prepared and ready to learn, but what does that mean? Pressure comes from well-intentioned groups, such as policy makers and administrators, to push academic curriculums for young children. Sometimes pressure comes from relatives, friends, and neighbors who have strong opinions about education. Stores are filled with educational toys to promote growth and learning in young children. Families are also influenced by mass, digital, and social media. The media has a powerful effect on parenting. Access to the internet and its extensive resources is growing daily. There is an abundance of educational literature and electronic communication through which parents can form online communities to share information, ideas, and other content. There are so many variations, directions, and ways to prepare children for the future that families are inundated with advice and uncertain what to believe. As early childhood education professionals, we know that the trend of teaching skills earlier and earlier is dangerous. Children need to be allowed to be children. They need opportunities to slow down, connect with others, and find internal motivation and their own interests. Life is about engagement with the world and finding meaning for you, whatever that may be.

LIMITED TIME

Time is something that we have little of in our busy lives. It seems as if there are always more tasks to accomplish than hours in the day. Families juggle work, chores, children's extracurricular activities, and other responsibilities. However, unstructured time is critical for reducing stress and refueling and for clarity, creativity, and autonomy. Time vanishes quickly when we are engaged in doing something enjoyable. Think of how fast time flies when you are immersed in reading a good book, watching a captivating movie, or spending time with friends. When your brain is absorbed in something pleasurable, you don't think about the passage of time. Children need long, uninterrupted blocks of time; greater time leads to greater complexity in play. Complex play scenarios and constructions can take hours or days to complete. In one New Zealand school, we observed fairy play that had been going on for several years, passed on from one generation of preschoolers to the next. Each new group of children continued to transform the fairyland by changing the kingdom, bringing treasures from home, telling tales, and creating gifts for the fairies.

Children learn through exploration and interaction with their environment. They maintain a high level of curiosity when they have ample time to explore, make decisions, and pursue interests. Children need an abundance of time to reflect and cultivate imagination. For children learning is intrinsically motivating. Children make meaningful connections through a spirit of wonder, joy, relationships, and play. Home environments provide the perfect opportunity to create spaces in which natural learning can flourish.

Consumerism envelops our daily lives. Children today are exposed to an enormous number of available products that are advertised directly to them on social media and television. Families may feel pressured to buy educational toys that claim to challenge children's intellect, stretch their imagination, and develop motor and social skills as preparation for school. Budgets are often tight, and families are often unable to afford expensive commercial toys that we would like to buy our children. While families have worthy intentions, a lot of purchased toys require little interaction and no imagination. They are fads that will not withstand the test of time. The great thing is that our homes are filled with items that are free, unique, and readily accessible, and that emphasize creativity. All you need to do is open a cupboard drawer to find materials that will spark a child's imagination and sustain their interest.

Remembering and Reclaiming Childhood

"I was seven years old when I first went to the greyhound dog track with my grandparents and cousin Becky. Most certainly the track atmosphere was not child appropriate, but times at the track were extraordinary for us girls. We were like Templeton the rat from Charlotte's Web *at the fair: the track was our smorgasbord. Becky and I sat cross-legged on the dirt-covered ground and collected hundreds of discarded race tickets. We were mesmerized by those cards. She and I organized, separated, stacked, and lined the castoff cards repeatedly. The cards became scrapers that we used to fan intricate designs into the dirt. We balanced cards on top of each other, creating mazes of structures. And when it was time to leave the track, we shoved piles of cards into our pockets to take back to Grandma's house, where we invented new games with them for hours and days on end. Interestingly we never did use the cards for their intended purpose of betting. I'm not sure what their appeal was, but I know that play with those cards entertained and satisfied our seven-year-old selves beyond all measure."* —Lisa Daly

Remember back to your own childhood and what captivated you. Was it making mud pies, running through the sprinklers, hunting for bugs, or playing flashlight tag? Often our childhood play involved risk, such as vaulting off a dirt-bike jump, fishing for pollywogs in a creek, or building a tree fort. And in most all instances, there was not any adult supervision of our risky endeavors. We were left unattended to travel in mixed-age packs of neighborhood children until dinnertime. For most of us, these times happened long ago, but the memories are deeply rooted and vivid as we recall the simple pleasures of childhood. One thing is for certain: throughout our childhood, we did not look on the internet to find fun things for kids to do during the summer. We automatically created our own play scenarios with found materials, such as discarded plywood, glass bottles, car tires, and wooden pallets.

Perhaps as adults we should slow down and take time to recall our fascinations with the simple items we played with as children and become filled with exhilaration, wonder, and inspiration once more. More than anything, childhood should be a time of exploration, engagement, and amazement. Shouldn't we want this type of joyful childhood for every child? Many parents and educators express powerful play memories as children, yet they seem to dismiss play's value and resist play experiences for their own children in favor of more structured activities. Children may be capable of learning scripted academic tasks, such as reading at an early age, but is it an advantage to do so? What is the cost?

Children need to be allowed to be children. They need spaces to run, jump, climb, hide, yell, make messes, and be creative. These are all important experiences for children, yet many children today have fewer opportunities to do what children are supposed to be doing. They live in more controlled and contained environments; have parents who are stressed, overworked, and tired; and experience rigid schedules and demands to meet academic standards. Reclaiming childhood is not an easy task with all of these pressures, but children still need a childhood rich in time, space, and open-ended materials to explore, wonder, imagine, investigate, and risk in order to thrive. These free, accessible, and intriguing open-ended materials that help children grow and reach their full potential through healthy play are called *loose parts*.

What Are Loose Parts?

Loose parts are materials that are open ended in nature. They offer children many ways to engage with them depending upon a child's experience playing with the materials. Because loose parts are nonprescriptive, they can be used flexibly. For example, a cardboard box may be used for building a tower, hiding inside, transporting materials, or creating a dollhouse or a dragon. In the classic book *Not a Box* by Antoinette Portis (2006), a box is not always a box. A box may be a robot, hot air balloon, fire engine, mountain, or race car, among many other things. Portis captures how an ordinary item transforms with the user's creativity. A closed material, by comparison, can be used only in a scripted way. For example, a puzzle has one way of going together, and a lifelike toy animal is difficult to imagine as anything but an animal. Closed materials may have the potential for building a child's sense of mastery, but because of their limited nature, children often become bored or frustrated with items that require no action on their part or that don't involve imagination. Children need materials they can act on. Do you remember letting your imagination run wild when you were a child and using found materials in unique ways? Perhaps you distinctly remember turning a large appliance box into a submarine, tunnel, hideout, or car wash. Perhaps you flattened the box and used it as a sled to slide down a grassy hill or turned it into a shield. Creativity requires only our imagination and open-ended materials.

Found or Inexpensive Materials

Most loose parts are materials found in home garages, drawers, cabinets, and nature. Garages can be filled with wood scraps, large washers, and bolts. Kitchen drawers contain pots, pans, and coasters. A storage cabinet may have fabric, ribbon, buttons, or towels. Nature is a source for pine cones, acorns, and driftwood. One of the best ways to obtain free loose parts is to ask family members and friends who may have unused treasures in their homes. Unexpected free materials, such as an empty electrical wire cable or protective cardboard rings that nest in between stacks of glass, can be found in store aisles. Inexpensive

loose parts can be unearthed at thrift stores, garage sales, and discount stores that sell interesting materials for a low price. Many communities have stores that collect remarkable found or discarded materials from local businesses and then sell items at discounted prices, often donating profits to a community cause. For adults and children alike, seeking out intriguing materials in unexpected places means rediscovering the complexity and beauty of the world around us.

Upcycled Materials

Loose parts are upcycled, sustainable items made from a wide variety of materials. They do not destroy natural resources, and they may be used over and over again, thus using our finite resources wisely and promoting positive, proactive, and effective personal choices and actions. An upcycled item is different than a recycled one. Recycling involves changing or treating items such as old paper, glass, cans, or plastic and turning them into new products so that they can be used again. Upcycling involves reusing an object for a new, innovative purpose. Examples include converting an old VCR rack to a weaving loom, turning a wooden shelf into a design pallet, or using a muffin tin to sort and organize sea glass.

The Origin of Loose Parts

The term *loose parts* is said to have been originally introduced by architect Simon Nicholson in 1971. He believed that everyone has the potential to be creative and inventive when given materials and opportunities to experiment, discover, and form new concepts. Nicholson offered us several insightful suggestions:

Loose Parts as Variables

Nicholson used loose parts to mean open-ended materials that can be used and manipulated in different ways. His definition of loose parts even extended beyond open-ended materials to include experiences with phenomena such as chemical interactions, gravity, motion, sound, wordplay, concepts, and ideas. Play possibilities and learning are endless in spaces that contain an unlimited variety of loose parts. Woodland Tribe, a nonprofit organization in England that promotes adventure playgrounds with loose parts, describes how children create "remarkable structures and spaces that are non-permanent, full of uncertainty and possibility, always playful, organically changing moment to moment, day to day" (Woodland Tribe, accessed 2018). However, many play spaces created for children are not like the ones described by Woodland Tribe. Instead they are clean and static, leaving few possibilities for children to use their imaginations and manipulate items as they desire.

Loose Parts and Space Design

Nicholson proposed that professional architects, designers, and builders who create children's play environments have all of the fun. While designing intriguing play spaces, they experience pleasure, creativity, satisfaction, and innovation as they determine locations, furnishings, and materials. As a result, they have stolen all the fun and creativity from the children. Children learn most readily and easily in an environment where they can joyfully investigate and discover things for themselves. They need open-ended materials and opportunities to shape the environments where they play.

A five-year research study of outdoor play spaces in Vancouver, British Columbia, found that "outdoor play spaces that contain materials that children could manipulate—sand, water, pea gravel, mud, plants, pathways, and loose parts offered more developmental and play opportunities than spaces that did not contain these elements" (Herrington et al. 2007, 10). The cotton-wool generation, comprised of the children and teenagers of the early twenty-first century, may not have had many opportunities to play in spaces they could manipulate because they were overprotected while growing up. Tom Williams, the founder of Woodland Tribe, states, "In our cotton wool society children are often not used to that amount of freedom and control. But we firmly believe that children build a stronger attachment to the space and their play is richer and more rewarding when they are actively involved in creating and changing it" (Woodland Tribe, accessed 2018). Adults can provide safe and creative spaces in the classroom and at home for children to create, construct, assess, and transform their own ideas through play with loose parts.

Types of Loose Parts

Loose parts are made from a variety of materials:

- natural (stones, shells, seedpods)
- paper (newspaper, boxes, cardboard tubes)
- metal (washers, keys, tin cans)
- plastic (cups, tubes, bottle caps)

- textile (ribbon, fabric, towels)
- wood (spools, molding, maple rings)
- glass (stones, napkin rings, sea glass)
- rubber/silicone (cooking utensils, cupcake molds, trivets)

Functions of Loose Parts

Loose parts can be organized according to an item's function:

- connecting (wire, string, clips)
- disconnecting (Velcro hair rollers, nuts and bolts)
- transporting (containers, bags, buckets)
- making noise (cans, spoons, gourds)
- rotating (egg beater, salad spinner, nuts and bolts)
- enclosing (boxes, tins with lids, crates)
- enveloping (blankets, scarves, towels)
- inserting (pipe cleaners, keys and locks, nesting bowls)
- cooking (utensils, pots and pans, bowls)
- plumbing and electrical supplies (pipe, fittings, wire)
- transforming (paint, dough, clay, water, sand, dress-up materials)

The Value of Loose Parts Play

Play is the most powerful source of enjoyment and active learning as an integrated process that brings together everything children learn, know, feel, and understand. When children engage in play with loose parts, they explore feelings, relationships, and ideas. The main ingredients for play are time, space, and materials that are simple, inspiring, and transformable—in other words, loose parts. In spontaneous, natural play, children are able to apply and grow in their personal experiences of novelty, risk, exploration, and practice. Trial-and-error learning with open-ended materials is the best form of play. When children are absorbed in learning, they will develop a deeper understanding of concepts. Free play enhances competency, promotes active learning, and supports development across the emotional, social, cognitive, physical, and creative domains.

Enhancing Competency

As children engage with loose parts, they are able to investigate new materials, build structures, create stories, make movements and sounds, sculpt models, create designs, and play various roles, either alone or with others. Through this kind of play, children are practicing and developing essential capacities:

- collaborating
- communicating
- coordinating movements
- critical thinking
- discussing
- engaging
- evaluating
- experimenting
- exploring
- focusing
- formulating
- investigating
- listening
- negotiating
- noticing
- persevering
- predicting
- problem solving
- questioning
- reflecting
- responding
- self-regulating
- wondering

Active Learning

Learning is profoundly integrated in young children; it involves all facets of the mind, body, and spirit. Children learn best when their whole being is actively engaged. They need to physically explore materials through their sense of sight, smell, hearing, taste, and touch to create meaning in their world. Loose parts are a critical component of active learning, as children can use the open-ended materials in any way they desire. Firsthand experiences build up the abilities, knowledge, and understanding that will support future learning. Active play with loose parts encourages, inspires, and supports children in their emotional, social, cognitive, and physical development; language, literacy, and communication; logical-mathematical thinking; and creative learning and development. Play with loose parts provides opportunities for children to acquire a positive mind-set, show understanding of newly acquired abilities and competencies, and strengthen learning.

Understanding how play with loose parts promotes and enhances children's growth and development will help guide you in selecting appropriate materials and experiences that will address children's needs. Loose parts are versatile, adaptable, and progressive, which makes them ideal for promoting learning and development. Their uses are endless. For example, a scarf can transform a child into a bride or superhero, or it can represent water in a play scene. Loose parts are also adaptable and progressive because they may be used at different levels in increasingly complex ways. For instance, clay can be used to pound, squeeze, and poke, but it can also be sculpted into a representation of a turtle as a child's confidence and ability to mold clay develops.

Emotional Development

Emotional development focuses on children's capacity to experience, process, and regulate emotions; form secure relationships; and build self-esteem and competency. Through play children gain emotional capacities in negotiating conflicts, delaying gratification, acquiring flexibility, living with disappointment, and developing empathy (Christakis 2016a).

Play with loose parts offers the opportunity for children to process their concerns, desires, and fears. It gives children power and control over materials and a way to master their circumstances and impulses. Children are able to conquer fears, confront challenges, resolve conflicts, and grasp confusing situations as they interact with responsive materials. For example, Laura's four-year-old daughter, Isabel, expresses concern over the fires near their home. To help her express her feelings, Laura places a variety of natural materials—sticks, leaves, acorns, and stones—on their patio table for Isabel to explore. She sits, observes, listens, and inquires as Isabel creates with them. Isabel places small stones in the center of the table and then covers them with twigs and leaves. She explains that fire was coming, and the animals needed to be protected. Play with the natural materials allows Isabel to explore her thoughts and emotions as she communicates her fear in a concrete way. Laura is able to talk effectively with her daughter after seeing and listening to her concerns revealed through play.

Social Development

Social development is the capacity to form secure relationships, understand other people's problems, engage in positive peer interactions, form friendships, have empathy, collaborate, and show concern for the welfare and rights of others. One of the main ways children develop socially is through their communicative skills in play and interaction with peers. Social language develops as children engage with loose parts and with teachers, relatives, family friends, and playmates. Social language includes such skills as joining and participating in group play; initiating, maintaining, and ending conversations; and maintaining appropriate body language and tone of voice—all of which develop in free play. As children explore, they learn awareness of others and how to understand and accommodate the perspectives of others. Through social-moral dilemmas that involve reciprocal interactions with their playmates, children learn to make informed choices about their behavior by factoring in the perspective of others (DeVries and Zan 2012). The ability to negotiate and collaborate develops as children decide who is going to play the role of the mom or the dog, or how to keep rushing water from collapsing the walls of their sand castle. Through interaction with peers who are supportive and capable of listening to one another's ideas, social competency builds. Concepts of fairness and equity are demonstrated as older playmates are supportive of including younger ones and assist the younger ones in finding and excavating rocks.

Cognitive Development

Cognition is the ability to think, reason, remember, and communicate. It encompasses symbolic play, problem solving, cause and effect, and spatial relationships. Children adjust their own understanding as they explore and learn about the world. Play with loose parts supports children's construction of conceptual knowledge as they manipulate and investigate the world around them. The development of abstract or symbolic thought is one of the significant aspects of cognitive development in early childhood. The foundation for abstract thinking is built in play as a child uses an object in a way that is increasingly different in form and function from the conventional uses of the object.

SYMBOLIC THOUGHT

Children often demonstrate symbolic thought through imaginary play. For example, they may have a plan to blast off in an imaginary space shuttle in their backyard. They may find a piece of plywood to be the launch pad, crates to be shuttle seats, an old computer keyboard to serve as the control panel, and a sheet to serve as the shuttle's drag chute upon landing.

PROBLEM SOLVING

Problem solving is our ability to assess the challenges of a situation and gather information to find a solution. A child's skill improves as he is able to recall previous experience and apply that knowledge when attempting to handle a new problem. For instance, children have to problem solve when deciding how to keep their feet from touching the imaginary lava on the ground, transport water across their yard, hold sticks together, or make a block structure stabler.

CAUSE AND EFFECT

Causation is the relationship between cause and effect, the ability to understand the connection of how things work. Grasping causal relationships is an important intellectual skill for children because it influences how they learn to assess whether their understanding is correct and valid (Galinsky 2010). Children make meaning and see connections through direct experiences, investigation, and discovery. They are innately curious and persistent as they engage with loose parts to try to understand and master information. For instance, as Bonnie pours water into a plastic pipe, she sees it flow out the other end. As she shakes a gourd, the dry seeds contained inside make a rattling sound. When she drops spoons from different heights, she sees how they fall and hears the noise they make when they land.

SPATIAL RELATIONSHIPS

Spatial conceptualization is the intellectual ability to understand how objects and people occupy, move in, and use space. Spatial concepts include spatial relationships, or the relative position of people and objects to each other in space. For example, a child may place a cardboard tube next to, under, on top of, in front of, or behind a fort that they are building in their living room. As children actively manipulate loose parts and their bodies, spatial understanding is strengthened.

Physical Development

Physical development focuses on physical growth and motor competency to control the muscles in our bodies and comprises large-motor, small-motor, and sensory-perceptual development. Large-motor development includes control of the large muscles in our arms, legs, and back to execute large body movements such as crawling, walking, balancing, running, climbing, and hopping. Small-motor development encompasses the use of small muscles in our fingers and hands essential for grasping, drawing, writing, and self-help skills such as feeding, zipping, and buttoning. Sensory-perceptual development involves assigning meaning to information that comes through the senses. Children use taste, touch, hearing, sight, smell, and kinesthetic senses to gain meaning from their explorations. Children's physical development is enhanced as they play with responsive materials that they can fill, dump, transport, transform, connect, and throw. Dexterity and strength are gained as children lift, transport, and stack rocks. Small muscles are strengthened as they pick up seashells to adorn each rock stack. Sensory awareness is developed as they handle the rocks, feel their texture, and note the weight, color, size, and shape of each rock.

Language, Literacy, and Communication Development

Language and literacy encompass listening, speaking, reading, writing, thinking, and observing. As children engage in play with loose parts, they develop receptive and expressive language, vocabulary, reciprocal communication and conversation, and symbolic representation. Children incorporate language and literacy into their play in a variety of ways. For example, Ian uses sticks to make the letters in his name. Sunitha's play involves the reenactment of going to a hospital for help. She makes the universal cross symbol of a hospital by crossing two bamboo sticks and wrapping them together with a shoelace and places it on a structure she has built.

RECEPTIVE LANGUAGE

Receptive language describes the ability to understand information that is spoken, while expressive language is the ability to communicate what is understood. Children need to have experiences to talk about so they can develop these skills. When we fill our homes and classrooms with intriguing loose parts, such as containers, fabric scraps, yarn, washers, tiles, and bottle caps, children have opportunities to create complex play scenarios. The materials can be combined and rearranged in multiple ways, and they can be used to represent other items. There is no limit to the possibilities. This is the case with Anjelica, whose grandfather recently passed away. With bottle caps and sticks, she creates a scene of her grandfather playing golf, his favorite sport, in heaven. Next, she uses the objects to depict an exceptionally large spider that was found in her bedroom.

Later the green bottle caps become frogs outside of her bedroom window that croak "too loudly" and keep her from falling asleep. Each time, Anjelica uses descriptive language to communicate her thoughts as she attempts to make sense of each situation. Since the loose parts are open ended, Anjelica can continue to use her imagination to make stories. Who knows? Perhaps the bottle caps will be food for her pretend rabbit tomorrow. Vocabulary increases rapidly in early childhood when children are exposed to rich conversation (Marulis and Neuman 2010), and children gain valuable language practice as they play with sounds and exchange ideas.

RECIPROCAL COMMUNICATION

Reciprocal communication involves engaging in back-and-forth conversation. Through play with loose parts, children develop the ability to talk about ideas and concepts, demonstrate turn-taking when talking and listening to others, and learn about the social use of language. Judith Van Hoorn, Patricia Monighan Nourot, Barbara Scales, and Keith Rodriguez Alward assert that "taking on the roles of different characters and sequencing events to tell a story form the foundation for the important aspect of literacy learning called narrative" (2007, 60). A narrative is a story or an account of connected events, real or imaginary, that are in a sequence. Narratives for younger children can be seen and heard in their play. Language is the key factor in children creating and sharing their narratives. Joel props a softball-size lump of clay on top of an irregular wooden tree branch block to represent a tree. He then places a pine cone on top of the clay that symbolizes a pterodactyl and several mini pine cones at the tree's base that are "babies." He tells his grandmother, Eleanor, an elaborate story of the pterodactyl's hurt wing, the "babies who can't fly 'cause their wings are limp," and how they all must escape from tyrannosaurus rex (a wooden clothespin) who is the enemy and is coming to eat all the babies.

SYMBOLIC REPRESENTATION

Symbolic representation, using one object to represent another, is a necessary prerequisite for learning to read and write. The language that we use to read and write is made up of symbols that are representations of thoughts and objects. When a child substitutes one item for another, such as using a rolled-up place-mat as a telescope or a pot as a hat, they demonstrate an understanding of the loose part as a symbol for the actual item they are imagining it as. An important early literacy skill is the ability to see similarities and differences between visual symbols (National Institute for Literacy 2009). When Hudson plays with sea-shells and sea glass, he notices similarities and differences in color, texture, size, and shape. Gaining such keen observation skills will help him distinguish differences between similar letters and word patterns when he begins to read.

Symbolic representation can also be expressed through sounds that represent a variety of objects and actions. Consider Kiho, who races and crashes a piece of driftwood that he has transformed into a car. He imitates the vroom of a car and the screech of car tires when the car brakes suddenly.

Logical-Mathematical Thinking

A critical look at children's cognitive capacities, particularly their numerical skills, provides a framework for understanding how children acquire logical and mathematical knowledge. Children first gain mathematical understanding through child-initiated, open-ended play experiences. As children interact with the physical world, they begin to construct understanding of many basic mathematical concepts, such as number sense, one-to-one correspondence, classification, patterning, ordering, and measuring.

NUMBER SENSE

Number sense is a person's ability to use and understand numbers. However, recognizing a written number and saying the number is very different than knowing what that number represents. That is, identifying the number five and counting to five is easy, but knowing what five means is challenging because it involves making a connection between quantities and counting. Five scarves look different than five buttons or five spoons, but they are all the quantity five. Number sense is a concept that children acquire as they engage in natural play. Preparing for a fun-filled day at the lake, Jayme's mom fills a beach bag with tin cans, buckets, pie pans, and metal spoons. Upon arriving at the lakefront, Jayme becomes absorbed in scooping spoonful after spoonful of dry sand into tin cans and then mixing in murky lake water. She says, "Hey, look, I made two milkshakes, one for you and one for me."

ONE-TO-ONE CORRESPONDENCE

One-to-one correspondence is the understanding that one group has as many items as another. Loose parts lend themselves to teaching one-to-one correspondence as children freely play with them. For example, Lupita places one eucalyptus pod inside each cup of a muffin tin as she pretends to make cupcakes. Later she lines up four feathers and puts one acorn directly under each feather.

CLASSIFICATION

Classification is the ability to group items together according to a common attribute, such as color, size, shape, or function. The ability to classify helps with organization. Think of your home and how items are grouped in your kitchen. Spoons, forks, and knives are clustered together, each in their own space, and there is a place on the shelves for cups, plates, and bowls. This arrangement helps us find things that we need with ease. Children naturally group items together in their play. A tin of buttons, for example, is perfect for children to sort.

PATTERNING

Patterning involves the making or discovering of auditory, visual, and motor regularities. Cheri places a basket of wooden thread spools on the living room shelf. The spools vary in size (small, medium, and large), and they are wound with five different colors of thread. Three-year-old Mia spontaneously plays with the spools. Without any adult coaching, she sorts them by color, counts them, and builds several patterns. A consistent pattern of red, green, red, green comes first, followed by white, black, yellow; white, black, yellow.

ORDERING

Ordering or seriation concerns the relationship between objects and the ability to place the objects in a logical order or sequence, such as from shortest to tallest or from lightest to darkest. Jacob's dad adds plastic measuring cups to Jacob's bathwater. Jacob, three years old, demonstrates an understanding of seriating by taking apart the cups and then nesting them back inside each other.

MEASURING

Measuring is assigning a number of units to some property of an object, such as length, area, or weight. Children's understanding of measurement begins in the preschool years as they begin to show an awareness that objects can be compared by weight, length, or capacity (Clements and Stephan 2003). During children's play, language may be used that illustrates an understanding of differences, such as describing things as lighter, shorter, or heavier. Children may also expand their knowledge of comparing by placing items side by side. While in the bathtub, Ruby learns about measurement as she pours water back and forth into different size cups. She watches to see which cup holds more and which holds less, and then shifts her interest to watching water spill over the edge of the cup.

Creative Development

Creativity is our ability to see things in new ways or combine unrelated things into something new. It involves flexibility in thinking and the expansion of ideas. Children's creativity is cultivated in rich home and classroom environments that encourage inventive thinking and offer exciting possibilities for investigation with intriguing materials. Creativity requires time and space, both indoors and outdoors, for children to tinker, design, communicate ideas, and express themselves. Imagination is having the capacities to create ideas, concepts, and images that do not exist. Children's creative development will be enhanced through handling, exploring, and experimenting with loose parts. Your home environment is a perfect laboratory for exploration, inquiry, imagination, and problem solving. Upcycled and natural materials lend themselves to unlimited possibilities. Consider Nathan, who makes music by drumming with spoons on inverted tin cans, wooden salad bowls, and plastic buckets. Later he pretends to make pancakes by cracking eggs (oak galls) into the wooden salad bowl, sprinkling on dirt, adding water, and stirring the batter with his drumming spoon.

Discovering and Collecting Loose Parts

Involve children in the discovering and collecting process. Remember that young children are interested in materials that they can change and use in different ways, so hunt for unrestricted treasures that you have around your house and classroom. Open up cabinet drawers and doors to unveil ordinary materials. Finds may include wire whips, spoons, napkins, coasters, ribbon, and felt scraps. A garage may have leftover materials from a project, like fence post caps, wood scraps, vinyl gutters, or drywall shims. Have children participate in collecting sustainable and recyclable materials such as tin cans, reusable containers, and paper towel rolls. Keep an eye out at stores for free materials as you wander up and down aisles; you may discover cardboard apple flats or cardboard cove molding. Take a stroll through your neighborhood or go on a nature hike. Go equipped with pockets or buckets, as everyday outings can yield surprising finds, including pine cones, eucalyptus pods, pebbles, and leaves. Engage family members and neighbors in your quest to find loose parts. Explain what loose parts are to grandparents, aunts, uncles, and friends. You will be surprised to see what items appear on your doorstep. Go to garage sales and thrift stores to buy secondhand items that can be repurposed for play. You will find yourself passing up toy selections and searching for unusual items that have more play potential.

Identifying Spaces for Loose Parts Play

First consider specific rooms where family and friends gather in your home, such as the kitchen, dining, family, and living rooms. Next think about spaces where routines and chores are done, like bathrooms, laundry rooms, and offices. Reflect on unusual and private spaces indoors, such as an entryway or hallway, under a table or stairwell, or a tucked-away corner. Any of these areas can be made into play spaces through the arrangement of loose parts in the space or the definition of the space with an area rug or a tray for items. A variety of loose parts can be added to each of these places for differing play experiences.

Going Outdoors with Loose Parts

Patios, decks, gardens, grassy areas, and secluded spaces outside are all ripe for loose parts play. Integrating materials like sand, water, and dirt into outdoor spaces lets children exercise control over materials and their play. A fascinating outdoor space can be created by repurposing a low table into a mud kitchen. Add pots, pans, bowls, water, dirt, and spoons for making concoctions. A tire, wheelbarrow, tub, or planter box can be used to create a sand area. Simply fill a large container with sand and add scoops and buckets for filling and dumping, or seashells and stones to bury and collect. A blanket and pillows are perfect for a cozy space to relax. Children can use loose parts placed in the space to create and tell stories or make designs.

Family outings and classroom field trips are additional opportunities for loose parts play. No advance preparation is needed because loose parts such as driftwood and rocks at a trip to a beach or pine cones, sticks, and rocks on a camping trip are often readily available for unlimited fun. You may want to consider packing a few loose parts on these getaways, such as buckets and shovels.

Organizing Loose Parts

Play materials in your home or your classroom can overwhelm the space and create a visual nightmare, or they can enhance the aesthetic elements that make these spaces warm and welcoming. Your home reflects your design style, values, culture, and family history; loose parts can offer similar visual appeal and function. To create a pleasing environment that complements your home's decor, surround yourself with beautiful loose parts and containers that bring you joy and reflect your culture. Infuse spaces with natural objects and authentic items rich in texture and color. Utilizing organizational strategies will help limit clutter. When arranging open-ended materials, study each space to see what can be used to contain loose parts. For instance, a low drawer or cabinet is perfect to house cooking utensils and containers in the kitchen and keep materials out of sight. Loose parts can be attractively stored on a bottom shelf or in a storage unit, placed in a basket or box, or displayed on a tray. Here are some ideas:

Containers

- storage boxes
- boxes with compartments
- baskets
- buckets
- shoeboxes
- crates
- tins
- tea chests
- jars with lids
- garden pots
- hanging baskets
- desk organizers
- letter trays
- flatware trays
- magazine files

Wall Hangings

- display shelves
- wall shelves/racks
- hooks
- shower baskets
- towel hangers/racks
- bed pockets
- magnetic boards

Furniture

- workbenches
- storage benches
- potting benches
- shelving units
- storage cubes
- TV units
- side tables
- coffee tables
- cabinets
- drawers
- shoe racks
- wine racks

Accessing Loose Parts

To promote independence, select spaces and containers that children can easily access on their own. Shallow, open containers provide visibility for children to see what's inside, and materials organized on low shelves or the floor are within children's reach. Avoid deep containers, as these can become junk traps with materials randomly thrown in. Such containers can make it hard for children to see and find what they need. Additionally, loose parts should be in the space where they will be used. For example, put pots, metal juice lids, and spoons in a low kitchen drawer that your child can pull out. Place rolled-up towels or small blankets in a basket next to your couch for fort building. An open tote of scarves and costume jewelry by a bedroom mirror is user friendly for imaginative play.

Avoiding Too Many Loose Parts

Too many loose parts can be overwhelming and overstimulating for children, families, and play spaces. Too few materials can frustrate children and limit their opportunities for play. The solution is to have just the right number of loose parts. A rule of thumb is to have more of fewer materials. Having a lot of the same material is better than little bits of many different items. For example, a large tub of bottle caps offers multiple possibilities for designing, sorting, patterning, and lining up and is better than a few bottle caps with a limited number of craft sticks and clothespins.

Considering the Play Possibilities for Loose Parts

Children want to play with responsive materials that can be transported, filled, dumped, collected, floated, dropped, inserted, and rolled. They are captivated by new opportunities. Think about what a child might do with available materials and add loose parts to create more play potential. For instance, if a child has access to a dish tub of water, they may splash it or pour it all out. If, however, you add some measuring cups, they will probably become fascinated for an extended period with filling the cups and pouring water. Their engagement can be further prolonged by adding a funnel or sieve to watch water rain down. If a child has two bowls of equal size, they may bang them together or try to fit one inside of the other, which may cause frustration. But if you add bowls that nest, their interest will shift to placing the bowls repeatedly inside of each other and then pulling them apart. Add a wooden spoon, and they can create sounds by banging the bowls with the spoon.

Assuring Loose Parts Are Safe and Healthy

Loose parts require special considerations when it comes to safety. Because loose parts are generally found materials, extra precaution is needed to assess safety factors, such as size, durability, material, and age-appropriateness. Adults are always responsible for protecting children from physical harm. Be aware of developmental differences. For example, an infant is more prone to place a small item in their mouth, which may be a choking hazard. Keeping children safe is a matter of common sense. Check to be certain that an item does not have small parts that can break off and become choking hazards. Never allow children to play with objects containing lead or other poisonous chemicals. Know, however, that children need to take risks to reach their full potential. Your home and classroom environments must challenge children without being hazardous. There is a difference between a risk and a hazard; a risk involves exposure to danger, while a hazard is a source of danger. Removing hazards but leaving elements that allow children to take risks is ideal. Remember that the best safety precaution is adult supervision.

Fostering Family Engagement

An early childhood educator has an important role in fostering family engagement by making family members feel welcome, regularly communicating with them, and creating an environment that honors each family's race, language, culture, and structure. Loose parts provide an excellent avenue for family engagement as invaluable connecting agents between home and school. Educators, family engagement specialists, and home visitors will find the information contained in this book to be particularly helpful in their work with children and families. The text is rich in ideas to share with families that will build connections, support learning, and deepen engagement. Families are often relieved to know that spending money on expensive toys is not necessary for their child to learn. They are delighted to find out that what they have in their kitchen cupboards and drawers are perfect educational toys. In our work with families, we frequently hear them comment, "That is how I played when I was a child. I never thought to give my child pots and pans."

We urge educators and family engagement specialists to introduce loose parts to family members during an adult gathering. Have adults play with the materials so they can experience the value of open-ended play firsthand. What did they learn or accomplish through their play with loose parts? Encourage family members to share critical-thinking dispositions they experienced while engaged with loose parts: curiosity, perseverance, flexibility, reflection, and collaboration. Provide lists of common materials that families may have in their homes or neighborhoods, and invite them to discover their own loose parts. Use this book as a family resource, as all photographs are taken in family homes and include common household items.

Family home visitors can uncover available materials in the home in collaboration with family members during home visitations. For example, if the home visitor brings playdough for children to explore, open cabinet doors and drawers to find a rolling pin, potato masher, or biscuit cutter. If a child finds insertion fascinating, look for nesting objects such as measuring cups or bowls. Cut an opening in the top of an oatmeal container or shoebox for a child to insert plastic bottle caps. On a future visit, bring pipe cleaners for the child to insert in the holes of a kitchen colander or plastic golf ball. Visits are a perfect opportunity to have a conversation with families about their children's interests and capabilities while the children engage with open-ended materials. Loose parts brought by a family home visitor can be left in the home to support and extend children's learning, and suggestions can be made for other home items to be used for play. Visitors can revisit the learning opportunities during their next visit and bring different loose parts to support children's fascinations.

Loose Parts for Encouraging Play at Home

- kitchen (measuring cups, bowls, utensils)
- bathroom (sponges, basters, cups)
- bedroom (stones, fabric, spools for storytelling)
- living room (blankets/towels for fort building)
- outdoors (sand, water, dirt, tin cans)

Asking family members to contribute loose parts to the classroom is another form of family engagement. Write a letter to family members about loose parts that you need for your classroom. Include a list of items such as wood scraps, container lids, old jewelry, keys, bottle caps, and ribbon. Give children a small paper bag and ask them to bring in odds and ends from home. Materials can be explored and organized and new possibilities or uses discovered. Children gain a sense of ownership and pride as they make contributions, and the request sends a message that their family is valued.

Consider writing a letter to family members about loose parts to consider for birthday or holiday gifts. Families may not think about giving a dish towel or silicone cupcake molds as a gift for an infant to bat or grasp, or homemade tree cookies for a preschooler to use for stacking or imagining. One time when her children were young, Lisa gave measuring cups, spoons, funnels, a tub, and a note to just add water as a gift for a child's birthday. The mom of the child later reported that she initially thought that the gift was rather strange but was delighted when her child persisted in filling and dumping water for an extended period on their back patio.

Our Hopes for You

We hope that this book brings you relief, comfort, reassurance, and encouragement in your work with children and families in an ever-changing world. We want you to understand that you do not need to spend a lot of money on expensive toys for your program to promote children's academic achievement. There are free options that offer multiple play possibilities to enhance children's intellectual growth that may provide even more learning value. Remember that what children need to be successful in life involves much more than intellectual skills. It involves the building of capacities in the emotional, social, physical, intellectual, and creative domains. Learning is holistic with young children and happens best through open-ended free play.

Our desire is for this book to fill you with inspiration, encourage you to look at ordinary items differently, and challenge you to infuse loose parts into early childhood environments. We invite you to discover the splendor and magnificence of natural, surprising, and sustainable objects that surround us. Embrace these loose part treasures as learning materials, and dedicate various indoor and outdoor spaces for both quiet and active play so that children may risk, connect, create, imagine, investigate, and innovate. Take time to be with children as they engage with loose parts, and enjoy the simple moments as children prepare for life.

As early childhood educators and parents, here is our advice for you:

- Slow down. Take time to relax and refuel. Children need you now.
- Simplify. Too many toys can be overwhelming, so take time to declutter closets and shelves, donate unused toys, and keep only items that have lots of play possibilities.
- Do what seems natural. Trust your own instincts and be confident in your choices. Do not be persuaded by outside influences that may be encouraging you to push children too fast and too soon. Remain an advocate for what is best for children.
- Enjoy every moment. Experience the delight of watching children, be present with them, and share treasured times, such as the first time they discover their breath on a frosty morning.
- Trust that children are capable and competent. Allow children autonomy to select and do things on their own.
- Love. Nothing says "I love you" more than time together that instills a sense of belonging. Create a classroom climate of belonging and connectedness.
- Reevaluate what is important. When you take time to consider what you really want for children, consider the skills and capacities that children need to thrive in life.

Part 2
Knowingness

Self-Awareness

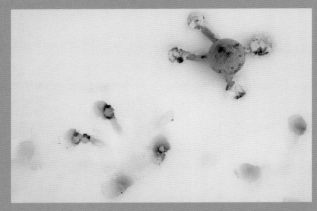

Critical Reflection

Adaptability

Identity

Self-awareness is our capacity to stand apart from ourselves and examine our thinking, our motives, our history, our scripts, our actions, and our habits and tendencies.

—STEPHEN COVEY

When children play in a new space or with loose parts, they experience it in their own unique way. Rather than focusing on the space or an object's intended purpose, children may view the experience in terms of affordances, or the properties of objects that define their possible use. US American psychologist James J. Gibson, one of the most important contributors to conduct research on visual perception, suggested objects have values and meanings unique to the person perceiving them. For example, an adult might understand a brick wall as a clear boundary between two areas. To a child, however, a brick wall can offer a place on which to walk, pile rocks, sit, balance, and jump (Gibson 1979). Loose parts support children's unique perceptions and affordances. They give children full control over the object, thus expanding children's ways of knowing.

When we consider the different ways children approach learning and understanding how their world operates, we begin to notice how insightful and perceptive they are. As we closely observe children engaged in play, we begin to see how they explore their feelings and thoughts. We also understand how hard they work to gain perspective on who they are and the people around them. For example, Alexis is a child with many ideas, and her mind is always creating and solving complex problems. At four years of age, she is a creative and insightful child. She knows what she can do, and she pursues her passions. Yet she struggles with giving space to other children's ideas. She instinctively knows that other children think differently, but in her own understanding, she sees her ideas as more important. In knowingness she is finding ways to communicate and listen to others. Because she has come to value her contributions, she is starting to understand that the input of others is also crucial. Through play and adult guidance, she will learn to channel her energy and give space to the ideas of other children. The ability to perceive feelings and emotions, including the wisdom that leads to empathy, is also crucial to knowingness. Arielle, at three years of age, is incredibly aware of other children's feelings. She observes, ponders, and responds with empathy and care. She is also cautious and takes time to make decisions that guide her, such as opting to enter play or choosing to stay behind. She knows when to engage in an argument and when to walk away. Both Alexis and Arielle are passionate and full of joy. They are exuberant and enjoy friendships and relationships with both adults and children. Their approach to knowingness is unique, and they require different levels of support and understanding. Their way of knowing will lead them to success in the future. More than likely they will encounter challenges, yet they will have the ability to solve problems and the resiliency and flexibility to maintain their curiosity and individual values.

Knowing and being able to express one's authentic self is important to the development of a child's identity. A sense of identity helps a child learn how to be themselves and promotes the development of a whole person who fulfills their full potential. Learning to be is the source of creativity and innovation. It helps a child gain the capacity to decide and act independently and to be an individual, a member of a family and community, a citizen of the world, an inventor, and a creative dreamer. Learning to be gives children the insight and creativity they need to function in the yet-to-be-created world of the future. Educating children goes beyond teaching them to read, write, and perform basic math; it involves giving them the life skills, knowledge, and disposition needed to be successful. Education needs to be infused with daily opportunities to reflect, test ideas, hypothesize, and solve complex social and intellectual problems.

Creating spaces and explorations at home that are dynamic and offer multiple opportunities to explore and engage in inquiry help children learn to adapt to change, build resiliency, and embrace flexibility. Both homes and schools can incorporate explorations that help children foster personal development of body, mind, spirit, creativity, and discovery. These play experiences can also encourage appreciation of the inherent value of the process versus the focus on the creation of a final product. Giving young children the opportunity to develop their own independent thinking and judgment allows them to make choices that will benefit them today and in the future. To better prepare children to be successful, education needs to incorporate every aspect of knowing: memory, creativity, reasoning, aesthetic sense, physical capacities, resiliency, intellectual learning, and social skills.

Playing with loose parts is a perfect vehicle to support the development of knowingness. The open-ended qualities of loose parts offer children every opportunity for aesthetic, artistic, scientific, and sociocultural discovery and experimentation. Loose parts transform learning from a merely utilitarian process into an active and engaging intellectual pursuit. When observing Roman, we notice that he enjoys building complicated structures using mini tree stumps and mini tree cookies. He often represents his home environment in his constructions. He is the only boy in a household of women, and he spends time exploring both gender roles. He is often seen using scarves to re-create a dress or long hair. He also uses a tool belt that he places on top of his makeshift dress. In his play, he is identifying with both gender roles; he knows that both genders are equally capable of engaging in complex interactions and developing mechanical skills to fix and create items. Roman has learned to respect women, and he tests what it is like to be female through play. His mother, grandmother, and aunt encourage his play. They want him to develop the capacities to nurture and be creative. His family realizes the importance of understanding the variety of possibilities loose parts play gives Roman.

Opportunities and Possibilities to Support Knowingness

- Offer children the opportunity to explore loose parts that bring an exploration of history into their play.
- Build on children's interests to explore and investigate new perspectives.
- Offer children open-ended materials that are flexible and support children in testing new ideas and hypotheses.
- Observe and listen to what children do and say. Ask questions that guide their learning process and give them deeper insight into how they know what they know.
- Focus on how children learn, not only on what they know. Go beyond teaching them letters, numbers, shapes, and colors. Instead support their learning dispositions and engage them in meaningful conversations about their interests.

CHAPTER 2
Self-Awareness

Self-awareness is having a complex understanding of one's personality, including one's strengths and weaknesses, thoughts, beliefs, emotions, and motivations. Humanistic psychologist Abraham Maslow (1987), in his hierarchy of needs theory, discussed the development of self-esteem and self-actualization. He introduced the idea that self-esteem and personal uniqueness develop from being unconditionally loved and accepted by families and communities. Human beings have the desire to excel and to be noticed for our unique talents and capabilities. Once we have acquired some measure of self-esteem and confidence, we gain the psychological freedom to be creative, to grow, and to be more generous with others. Maslow also argued that people have the desire to attain self-fulfillment, or the need to become everything that one is capable of becoming.

One important role of families is to create opportunities for young children to gain self-confidence and pride in their work and achievements. In comparison to playing with commercially manufactured toys, which have a predetermined purpose and outcome, children who play with loose parts are in full control of the outcomes. Loose parts play encourages children to recognize their own capacities and to reflect on their own power to exert change in their lives. Observe children at the beach or on a walk in nature. They can spend a long time exploring driftwood, sand, and rocks. They find and collect interesting rocks, intentionally using them in play. They arrange the loose parts in a combination of ways to depict castles, buildings, and entire cities. Children are in full control of their creative capacities. When they build with blocks, cardboard packing tubes, calculator tape cores, or wood tree cookies and tree stumps, they explore their abilities and recognize that they are capable and competent. This competence is emphasized when children often say after achieving a goal, "I am the bestest." There is nothing better than having that great sense of accomplishment to acquire self-awareness and self-knowledge.

No, Goose, No!

Two-year-old Cassidy and her parents spend a lot of time together at a pond situated in the middle of their neighborhood. At the pond, Cassidy enjoys walking around the water's edge, digging in the sand, collecting natural treasures such as leaves and sticks, and shooing the geese away. Each of these experiences helps her gain understanding of her capacities. One late October afternoon, her mom decides to have an outing to the pond before dinnertime. She brings a collection of Great-Grandma's cooking utensils for Cassidy to explore in the sand. As Cassidy focuses on filling an old flour sifter with sand, a curious goose persistently attempts to get too close for Cassidy's comfort. Cassidy holds up the spoon

in a warning pose and shouts at the goose, "No, goose, no!" She is learning that she is an individual separate from others who can assert herself, and that her words have power.

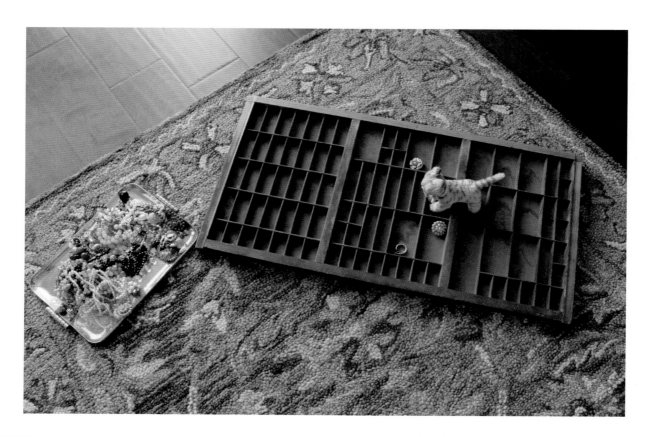

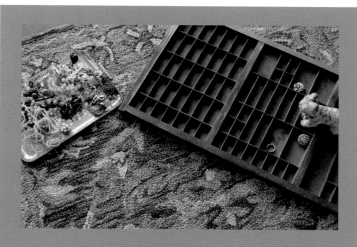

Grandma's old earrings and necklaces are treasures for Arielle to sort through. She enjoys touching and looking at the wide variety of clip earrings and gems. As she sorts through the pieces, she thinks about who she might be if she were to wear long dangling blue ones or pearls—a dancer or a princess perhaps.

Cassidy places sycamore balls one at a time into each open mold of a muffin tin. As she drops the eighth ball into the mold where she placed the seventh ball, she pauses. She looks at the two balls in one space, removes one, and places it in the remaining empty mold. Now there is one ball in each of the eight molds. Cassidy is gaining confidence in her abilities as well as learning possible uses for sycamore balls and an understanding of a math concept—one-to-one correspondence.

CHAPTER 3
Critical Reflection

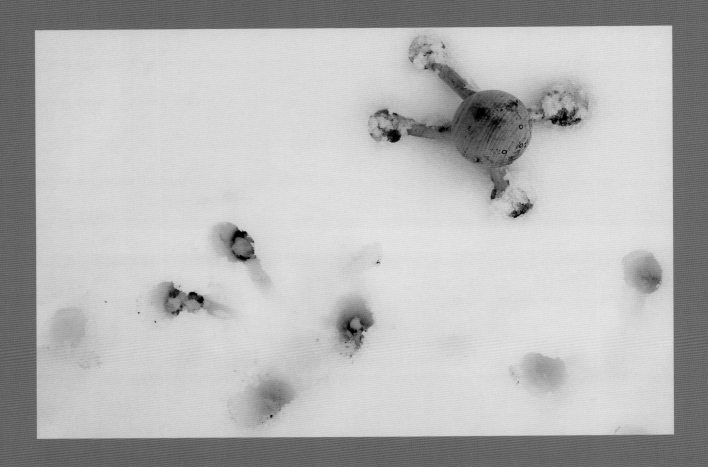

In the powerful process of exploration, children take the time to reflect and make sense of what is happening around them. The ability to reflect will help them be intentional in future endeavors. They will be able to analyze, hypothesize, and make informed decisions. For example, Jacob enjoys building and invites the neighbors to create different playscapes in his backyard. He combines milk crates and fabric and also incorporates the existing trees. He and his friends spend many hours in complex imaginative play, and every night he goes to sleep tired and full of joy. He has a sense of awareness of his own capacities, and he shares his knowledge with other children. The next day, he wakes up and, after breakfast, runs to the yard to continue building and making changes to his structure. He has reflected on what other materials he needs. He picks up paper and a pencil and in pretend writing creates a list that includes drawings. He proceeds to walk around the house finding the rest of the loose parts and other materials he needs. Critical reflection allows us to make meaning of our work. It helps us set goals and use our past knowledge and experiences to inform future decisions. Through critical reflection we can consider the real-life implications of our actions. Critical reflection is the link between thinking and doing. When children are taught how to reflect and consider their thinking and actions, they can experience a transformative process of learning.

The Imagination Trunk

One of the most treasured activities in Miriam's house was to explore the imagination trunk. Her daughters and their friends spent many hours playing with the scarves, beads, hats, bracelets, and wide variety of loose parts inside. They would use the contents to create complex dramatic play sequences. They would put on theater productions and use

 metal washers as entry tickets. Other times they would drag the trunk to the backyard to create fairy worlds. The fairies were made from wooden clothespins and pieces of fabric. Scarves would serve as lakes and rivers that surrounded the fairylands. They would go on walks around the neighborhood to gather pine cones, acorns, and liquid amber balls.

They would also take wine corks that had been collected in a glass jar in the living room. These items became houses for the fairies. The trunk was a staple in our household, and the children played with its contents for years. One of the most enjoyable parts was how our extended families and friends contributed to the trunk on a regular basis. They would donate tin cans, plastic lids, bottle caps, buttons, and many other intriguing and creative loose parts. The children's interest was piqued with every new addition. Each play scenario with items from the imagination trunk provided Miriam's daughters with the opportunity to examine and question ideas, values, and concepts. Through critical reflection, they sought to understand their actions, analyze their experiences, and derive new meaning.

On a frosty December day, Bonnie actively investigates the properties of rocks, pine needles, pine cones, and leaves in the snow. She strokes the long, thin pine needles and then uses them to brush the crusted snow. Her exploration provides opportunity for her to reflect and make meaning of how to use each natural material.

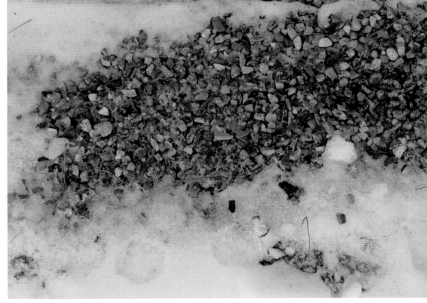

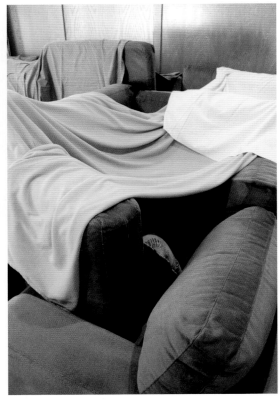

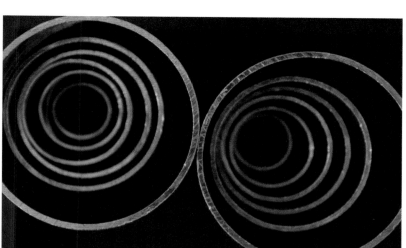

CHAPTER 4

Identity and Learning to Be

During the early childhood years, children begin to develop a sense of identity and self-concept. They recognize the attitudes, abilities, physical characteristics, and values that define them. By eighteen months to three years of age, they develop their Categorical Self, which is a concrete way to perceive themselves (Oswalt 2019). For instance, children assign themselves labels in terms of age ("I am three and a half"), physical characteristics ("I am strong"), and gender ("I am a boy or a girl"). As they continue to grow, they begin to define themselves in terms of feelings and interests: "I am happy and want to play with Jossie." As children begin to perceive societal expectations, they form relationships through play that contribute to their emotional, social, and cognitive development. As long-term memory develops, children incorporate their memories as they re-create their life history. They explore cultural and family values and begin to think of themselves as a member of the family and, later on, as a member of the community. When they gain metacognition—the capacity to know that they have ideas and thoughts—they develop an inner self. The inner self allows them to have private thoughts, feelings, and desires that nobody else knows unless they choose to share that information.

Families and educators can share children's history and values to support their identity. They can help children explore their identity by creating self-portraits using loose parts such as rocks, sticks, acorn caps, and other natural materials. Using the children's photos as inspiration can deepen their own understanding of who they are. Children learn from their culture, history, traditions, and family and community values. Families can provide opportunities to work together on art projects, such as collecting bottle caps and arranging them into an ongoing family collage. Going on a community walk in local parks, exploring stores, or searching garage sales are other avenues for discovering loose parts while learning about the community around them. These activities help children gain a deeper understanding of their identities as members of a family, culture, and community. When family members share their own collections, they provide children with a sense of history.

Great-Aunt's Buttons

Niqui enjoys going to her great-aunt's house. She always asks to play with the button collection. The buttons sometimes are used to create complex works of art. Other times she takes a muffin tin from the kitchen and sorts and classifies them by size, color, and shape. As she plays with the buttons, she asks questions about where the buttons

came from. She is curious about how old the buttons are and when her great-aunt acquired them. She loves hearing the stories of the different buttons and how they ended up in the box. Her great-aunt takes time to share what she remembers, and other times she makes up stories that she knows Niqui will love to hear. In playing with the buttons and sharing together, Niqui is gaining a deep sense of self and increasingly understands how she is a part of a family. She knows that she has her family's unconditional love, and that she is free to play, explore, and ask questions.

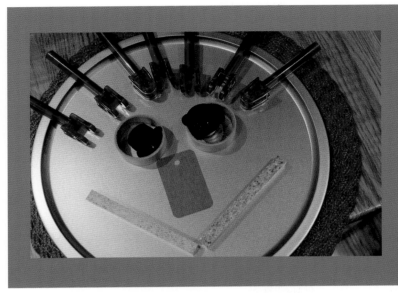

Plastic odds and ends, tiles, laminate samples, and cardboard rings offer Jason an opportunity to create his self-portrait. He glances in the mirror at his own features and then adds red spiky hair. He changes facial expressions as he explores his identity.

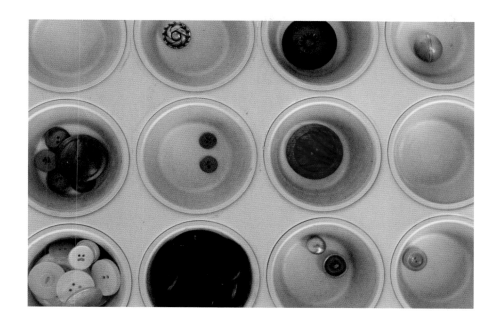

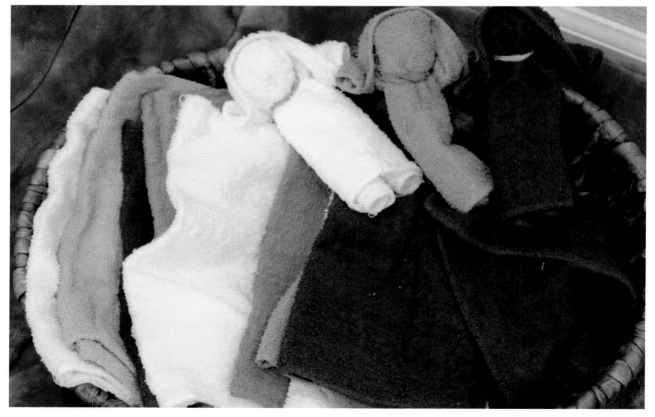

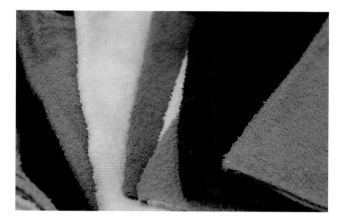

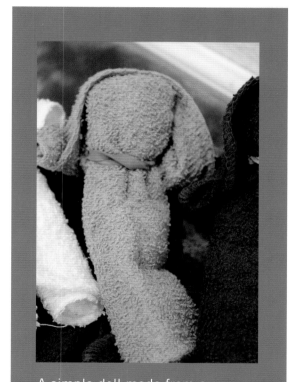

A simple doll made from a washcloth is perfect for carrying and cuddling. The doll is easy to grasp, carry, and hug. Skin-colored washcloths allow Chelsey to recognize that people are unique and have different skin colors.

CHAPTER 5

Adaptability and Resilience

Change, uncertainty, and novelty are realities of life. Children need resilience, the mechanism that helps us survive adversity and recover from even the most hostile situations. Resilience requires the capacity to be adaptable and flexible, critical skills that are understood as appropriate cognitive, behavioral, and/or affective adjustment in the face of uncertainty and novelty. To navigate the ever-changing world, young children will need to be adaptable and have the flexibility to explore and embrace diverse perspectives and possibilities.

Children who are able to think about a problem in a new way engage in flexible thinking. Playing with loose parts presents constant opportunities for flexibility and adaptation. This type of open-ended play allows children to solve problems, engage in positive peer interactions, and eventually focus on academic endeavors. When children learn to shift their thoughts in the face of new information, they can work through changes and transitions. Adaptability and flexibility improve with learning and development. The more children have, the more options they have for confronting novel changes. For example, as Alex plays with different fabric swatches and napkin rings, he can insert more than one swatch into a napkin ring as long as the fabric is thin. When he selects a thick fabric swatch, at first he struggles to make it fit into the napkin ring, then eventually finds a ring with a larger opening through which the fabric fits. He continues to switch the fabrics and napkin rings, exploring multiple possibilities. Later in the week, he is observed comparing the thickness of the material by lining up the swatches against blocks of different sizes. He stacks the fabric as he counts. With loose parts and flexible thinking, he is able to explore different units of measure.

Cooking Together

Shelby and Mikaela enjoy spending time playing outdoors. They are neighbors and often spend time in the courtyard between their apartments. Shelby's father has created a make-shift mud kitchen using an old shelf and low wooden cabinet. The kitchen has a variety of real utensils, pots, pans, and a tea set. The two friends look forward to cooking together.

They mix dirt, mud, and water to make mud cakes. They talk about the different things they are cooking for each other. Shelby's favorite food is macaroni and cheese, while Mikaela enjoys jambalaya. They walk around the courtyard collecting leaves, rocks, and unripe oranges, which are a bright waxy green, to add their cooking. They often discuss which dish tastes better as they pretend to eat, and they give each other advice and suggestions on how to improve. There are times when they argue about what to add and who cooks each dish. This gives them the opportunity to listen to each other, defend their dish, but also agree that they can both be great. In this scenario, the children have engaged in cognitive flexibility.

Sophie discovers that the strings of crystals are not easy to bend and shape into a necklace as she desires. She adjusts her original thought and shifts to draping and designing with the dazzling gems. Sophie's actions demonstrate how to be flexible when a problem occurs.

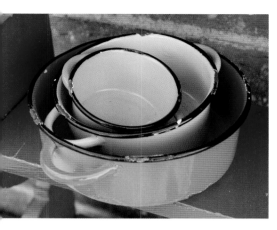

Part 3
Connections

Belonging

Communication

Empathy

Collaboration

Vulnerability is the birthplace of love, belonging, joy, courage,

empathy, and creativity. —BRENÉ BROWN

Take a moment to consider all the connections you make in your day-to-day life. When you are planning and organizing your day, you need to decide which task is more important and why. You connect the information that helps you decide how to prioritize. Connections are made even when completing simple tasks like selecting a container for storing leftover food. As adults we make connections in our work, daily life, and even in the relationships we have. Making connections plays an essential role in the development of the frontal cortex of the brain, and these connections are also a precursor for learning and creativity (Galinsky 2010). Making connections involves thinking, classifying, sorting, analyzing, and decision making. These are skills needed as children enter school and begin to engage in higher-order academic learning.

Making connections begins early in infancy. Babies not only recognize people when they see them, but they connect with them in special ways. They recognize different voices and smells. Infants also begin to make cause-and-effect connections. Observe infants the moment they first discover their hands. At first it is a random movement, and eventually, when they realize they have control over their hands, they start to reach for a mobile or an object placed in front of them. There is no better description of a cause-and-effect exploration than when an infant drops an object from their high chair and waits for an adult to pick it up. For the adult, the activity seems meaningless, but for the infant, the activity is filled with learning connections. They are exploring what happens when the object falls (gravity) and how far the object rolls (distance, but more importantly they are exploring the power of their actions as they see the adult's reactions. This type of play is fairly sophisticated and demonstrates how infants make connections that give meaning to the world they live in.

In the landmark report *From Neurons to Neighborhoods: The Science of Early Childhood Development* from the Institute of Medicine, scientists, theorists, and child-development experts determined the importance of creating environments that support making neurological, cognitive, and social connections for young children (2000). Neurological connections are forming from the moment of birth. In the first decade, a child's brain forms trillions of connections or synapses. Axons connect to dendrites, and chemicals called neurotransmitters send messages across the synapses. This process is mind-boggling, especially when we consider that by the time a child is three, fifteen thousand neurons are connecting to create a complex network of pathways that support learning and help the child make sense of the world. For an infant's brain to make neuronal connections, it needs positive and engaging connections with caring adults. As long as the brain continues to be stimulated, neuronal connections will continue to develop.

Neuronal connections continue to grow as children make further cognitive connections, which are best described through the lens of psychologist Jean Piaget's cognitive development theory. In this theory, he explains that children make sense of objects or situations in terms of schemas. A schema is related to both the physical and mental actions involved in knowing. Children place new knowledge in the context of existing knowledge. As children have new experiences, they modify, add, or change the previously existing schema. In this way, they make important connections that support their understanding of how things work. For example, when a child rolls a ball down a ramp, they become aware of how fast the ball rolls. However, they may associate speed with the color of the ball, rather than incorporating other possibilities. As they continue to explore speed, they may gain further understanding that how fast the ball rolls has little to do with its color and more to do with its weight and the incline of the ramp. When children make early connections about how things work and function, they gain knowledge of specific scientific concepts.

Families and educators alike aspire for children to make meaningful social connections. Play provides these opportunities. Making connections with other children is central to social well-being and helps children develop capacities to grow and sustain friendships, cooperate, lead, follow, and express their needs and feelings. Unstructured active play with others, including with parents, siblings, and peers, is a major opportunity to cultivate and sustain social connections.

Children also make connections through past experiences. They connect these past experiences to new knowledge. Children use their entire bodies to learn. They have an intrinsic need to see, touch, feel, smell, and hear everything that is happening around them. Before they can internalize and comprehend specific concepts, they need to engage in hands-on exploration. Learning from previous experiences is at the core of constructivism, a theory that focuses on observation and inquiry. This theory is based on the concept that children construct knowledge and understanding of the world through experiencing things and reflecting on those experiences. Constructivist education uses children's innate curiosity about how things work. It also supports the idea that children use previous experiences to build new knowledge. Educational philosopher John Dewey (1916) called for education to be grounded in real experiences found in children's local communities. To further support children in making meaningful connections, they need to be given the opportunity to construct knowledge by creating hypotheses, testing them, and coming up with their own answers and conclusions. Therefore, supporting children in making experiential connections needs to take priority in all our interactions.

Because loose parts are open ended by nature, they give children the opportunity to be curious and wonder about how things work and what kinds of connections can be made with the materials.

Opportunities and Possibilities to Support Making Connections

- Give children opportunities to reflect on specific problems they encounter and express their thinking and ideas in multiple ways, such as talking about them, depicting them using loose parts, or drawing them.
- Provide different loose parts and other materials, such as paper, colored pencils, and markers, for representing and recording their observations. For example, they may draw their observations and ideas or create a collage.
- Plan for time to talk with children, such as a family reflection time at the end of the day, and help them make meaning from their experiences.
- Build on prior knowledge. Think about other learning experiences children have had before and help them connect previous experiences to new ones. Use family outings and conversations as a starting point.
- Provide loose parts that exist for more than one purpose. Blocks can be stacked, sorted by color, placed in piles by size, and lined up, or they can represent other things like built structures. During bath time, use loose parts to explore concepts related to floating and sinking.

CHAPTER 6
A Sense of Belonging

Early in life, children begin to explore the meaning of belonging. They want to know how they are connected to other people. They will ask questions such as, "Are you my mommy because you take care of me?" Humans have an innate need to belong that makes up the core of feelings of well-being, motivation, and participation. Humanistic psychologist Abraham Maslow considered belonging such an important part of life that he placed it above the psychological need for safety in the hierarchy of needs. Children's sense of who they are is shaped by their characteristics, their behavior, and their understanding of themselves, their family, and others. In children's lives, friends and members of their community play a key role in building their identities.

A sense of belonging emerges through the meaningful connections children make with people, places, culture, and groups to which they belong. In "A Pedagogy for Ecology," Ann Pelo (2009) states that the role of educators is to give children a sense of place—"to invite children to braid their identities together with the place where they live by calling their attention to the air, the sky, the cracks in the sidewalk where the earth busts out of its cement cage." She further explains that children need to be invited to participate in the unfolding life of that place. In other words, belonging is about people feeling needed, wanted, and valued by other people, groups, organizations, environments, or spiritual dimensions. Social and emotional well-being is closely linked to our capacity to enjoy life and cope with stress, and it is also connected to feeling productive, appreciated, and loved. Experiencing unconditional love helps children develop a sense of belonging. As their sense of belonging increases, children grow up to be emotionally strong, self-assured, and capable of dealing with challenges and difficulties. Having a sense of belonging and receiving messages of respect, love, approval, and encouragement empowers them to develop a positive sense of who they are and a feeling that they make an important contribution to the world. When children receive positive messages about their families, backgrounds, cultures, beliefs, and languages, they develop pride in who they are. These messages also give them the confidence to voice their views and opinions, to make choices, and to help shape their own learning.

Autumn Leaf Piles

"City of Trees" is a nickname for several cities around the world, including Sacramento, California. The city's tree canopy is dense with oaks, sycamores, cottonwoods, walnuts, and elms, along with many other species. In the fall, yards are covered in thick blankets of leaves. Children, friends, and neighbors rake leaves into huge piles that line the streets' curbs for citywide collection during leaf season in November, December, and January. The leaf piles beckon

Evelyn and Emma, who walk around their whole neighborhood testing each pile. The sisters scoop up armfuls of leaves, throw them up in the air, and gleefully watch them rain down on top of them. They laugh as leaves crunch beneath their stomping feet. Evelyn is the first to take a plunge and belly flops into an irresistible leaf pile. Her whole body disappears underneath the leaves, and crawling through the leaves like a dog now becomes her new focus. A neighbor walking down the street stops to watch the girls frolic in the leaves. She smiles widely and says, "I remember jumping in the leaves when I was little. There is nothing better!" Many of us have fond childhood memories of playing in leaves, and this simple shared experience creates a sense of belonging within a community and across generations.

Bath time is a beautiful moment when children relax and enjoy playing with loose parts. Plastic measuring containers provide opportunities for children to watch the water dynamics as they fill and slowly pour out water into the tub. Nonslip stickers and plastic rings offer children opportunities to create exciting designs in the bathtub. Bath time is a time to connect and laugh together while following important routines that sustain a relationship.

CHAPTER 7

Children as Skillful Communicators

From birth infants have a desire to communicate and express their needs. They express their desire to connect with others through simple vocalizations. This capacity to communicate develops as children interact with one another, caring adults, and other people in their environment. Children's communication skills grow rapidly in the first five years of life. When an adult responds to children's body language and their attempts to communicate, they are supporting the development of a skillful communicator. Samuel, who is three, has been playing with antique wooden spools that his mother has collected. He shares with his mother that he likes the way some of the spools smell, as some of the spools are made of rosewood, but does not like the texture of some of the spools. His mother listens patiently and prompts him with some inquiry questions. She waits for his answers and then shares some of her ideas about the way the spools smell. Samuel is learning that what he has to share is important to the people who love him. He knows that he is a good communicator.

Loose parts are a perfect vehicle to engage children in meaningful dialogue and to help them make connections that expand their understanding of the world. When our view of children shifts from "we need to get them ready for the next stage of their life" to recognizing their current capacities, we will be able to give them the support they need to apply their current knowledge and continue to explore.

Young children are skillful communicators. They can tell us the story of their own lives from their personal perspective. When we listen to and focus on what children are telling us, we can gain tremendous knowledge about their thinking and perceptions. Part of communication is the ability to hear and listen to others' perspectives. When adults listen with close intent to what children are saying, they are modeling the important skill of listening. Babies start listening and reacting to noises, sounds, and voices at a very young age. By the time they are four months old, a baby will turn toward the sound of a voice. As children grow, they learn to listen to different sounds and voices and discriminate between them. Listening to music and banging along with pots and pans gives children a sense of rhythm and helps them recognize tone and melody. Toddlers love dancing and moving to music. Give them scarves and soft fabrics to incorporate into their dances. Young children enjoy singing for the pleasure of singing. They are confident about their ability, and most are eager to let their voices be heard. Wooden dowels, wooden containers, and wooden spoons can become drums to play as they sing. Children like songs that repeat words and

They also enjoy songs that use rhythms with a definite beat and those that ask them to do things. Young children enjoy nursery rhymes and songs about familiar things like animals, play activities, and people. Give them loose parts, such as rocks, tree cookies, empty containers, and felted animals, to re-create the nursery rhymes that interest them. Create sound gardens in your house that allow children to listen to interesting sounds. Simple household items, such as spoons and forks suspended from a tree branch, can create beautiful sounds as they are moved by the wind. Children learn early on to determine the origin of the different sounds; they distinguish between the sound the wind makes or how thunder roars. The more opportunities children have to listen to a variety of sounds, the stronger their ability to hear and listen will be.

Hallway Alley

A typical summer day in Colorado starts out with a sunny morning, but afternoons can be quite a different story. Clouds that appear on the mountains and foothills to the west develop into thunderstorms out on the plains. The sky darkens and then opens, and buckets of rain pour down. Flashes of lightning light up the sky. Sharp, loud cracks of thunder follow the flashes. Lisa's house lights flicker and then go out. That's when the fun begins. On these afternoons, flashlights,

blankets, sheets, and pillows come out for fort building. You can build a fort anywhere, but it works best at my house to create a cozy hideaway by the couch because we have all those cushions. On this stormy day, however, my mom has another idea. She turns our hallway into a bowling alley. What mom does that? Armed with rolling pins and balls, we set up pins and begin our game. Oliver holds the flashlight. Jenny takes the first turn and throws the ball with all her might toward the pins. The ball ricochets off the walls like it would off bumpers in the gutters of a bowling lane, and the wayward ball heads toward the pins. After three more throws, all the pins have toppled. My job is to reset the pins after they're all down. The lights come back on, but our game continues.

Throughout their play, the siblings actively talk to each other. Jenny tells James to watch out when the ball races swiftly down the hall. All three children make a crashing sound as the pins fall, and cheer each other on. Strategy is discussed to determine which technique is best to hit the most pins. James keeps score and announces who is in the lead after every roll. All of the children are familiar with the roles they play and are able to expand their play by offering suggestions and acting out realistic scenarios. Their communication skills expand as they listen to one another's ideas and respond to them appropriately.

A collection of antique spoons can engage children's curiosity and invite them to ask questions about the spoons' origins and provenances. They enjoy listening to stories about each spoon and taking turns describing the different details and designs.

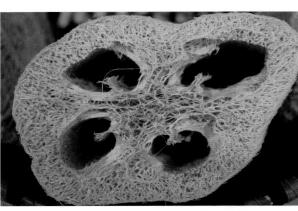

CHAPTER 8
Building Empathy

Empathy requires an understanding of your own feelings and the feelings of others. Empathy is closely linked to self-concept, which is defined as an overarching idea we have about who we are physically, emotionally, socially, and spiritually. Think of infants in a hospital nursery; when one infant cries, their crying triggers crying in other infants. This type of crying, even though it may only be triggered by a loud noise, is the precursor of empathy. Toddlers begin to show empathy in their first efforts to connect to another person's discomfort with their own. When two-year-old Sean sees Jeannea crying, he offers her a toy he's been playing with. In this action, he is giving Jeannea something that he knows has made him feel better when he has cried. Unclear, however, is whether Sean understands what Jeannea is feeling or is simply upset by the way she is acting, but he is on his way to developing empathy.

Empathy is a skill that is learned as children interact with both adults and peers. When children develop empathy, they tend to do better in school, in social situations, and in their careers as adults. Children who have the greatest capacity for empathy are viewed as leaders by their peers. As children's interactions with peers grow, they need to navigate increasingly challenging interactions. Family members and educators can help children learn empathy as they genuinely acknowledge and share their own feelings. For example, when an adult says to a child, "I am feeling sad that Grandma left to go back home," the child begins to understand that feelings are valuable and that they have the right to have strong emotions. Talking about how another child feels helps connect feelings to actions, and children begin to understand how their actions affect others. Saying to a child, "Oscar is crying because someone took away his blanket, and that makes him sad. What might make Oscar feel better?" is a good example of giving children room to express and connect with their feelings. Distracting them to avoid tears will interfere with the development of empathy. As they play with loose parts, children learn about cause and effect, and they begin to make connections to how their behavior affects others. Loose parts play offers children multiple opportunities to interact with other children and to express empathy.

The Dog Rescue

Donned with capes made from scarves, Joey, Lamar, and Tonya act out a rescue mission play scenario to save dogs that are trapped in cages. Their stuffed animals are stuck inside eucalyptus cages they built. They talk about how the dogs feel being trapped against their will by bad guys, demonstrating their compassion and ability to understand the feelings of another being. As they plan the rescue, they consider challenges they may encounter, including how they are going to feed the dogs and keep them quiet during the rescue, to prevent the bad guys from catching them. They take turns leading the planning and devising different solutions to their challenges. This account may seem like a simple play moment,  but it takes the children a long time to create a usable, comprehensive plan. They consider the importance of helping the animals and why it is important to do so. Their conversation is intense, and their ideas are thoughtful and always focused on the social justice act of saving the dogs. Listening to their conversation, you can hear themes of empathy, compassion, morality, and fairness emerging.

Spending quiet time sorting and classifying thread spools gives children the opportunity to reflect and connect to their feelings and emotions. Solitary play is important. It nurtures creativity and exploration and helps children learn to be comfortable being alone with their own feelings so that they might be more attuned to other children's feelings when they play in groups.

CHAPTER 9

Collaboration and Moral Development

Harvard child psychiatrist Robert Coles (1997) cautioned that we are making a grave mistake if we think of children's moral development as following external rules supplied by adults. He argues that "moral intelligence" is not acquired only by memorization of rules and regulations or expected compliance. We grow morally as a result of experiences that teach us how to interact with others and how to behave in this world. According to Coles, following rules for the sake of obtaining a reward does not foster the same intrinsic satisfaction as following a rule for the greater good. It does not cultivate the ability to empathize or behave morally in the future. Play is intrinsic to moral development, for in play children learn to respect and appreciate the boundaries that rules bring to interactions. Children also begin to acknowledge the deeper meanings of moral behavior through play. Morality includes a sense of justice, compassion, and caring about the welfare of others as well as perspective-taking, the ability to discern how someone might be thinking or feeling.

A moral sense of "goodness" emerges through a variety of social interactions, children's own thinking about these experiences, and a dialogue with adults and peers about the situation. As children engage in collaborative loose parts play, they begin to gain an understanding of how other people think, behave, and interact with each other. They make connections between different cultures and ways of being in the world. They also gain awareness and explore how to successfully maneuver different social challenges. As they negotiate and collaborate to complete different projects, they develop a deep understanding of what society expects of them. In open-ended play, children learn to understand and negotiate social rules and acquire moral thinking in many scenarios:

- taking turns as they play together
- cooperating as they trust and develop friendships with other children
- respecting and accepting others
- understanding and respecting boundaries
- negotiating to get their ideas heard and their needs met
- solving problems and coming up with innovative solutions
- learning how things connect through cause and effect

Alien Bert and the Carrot Nose

It is the first snowfall of the season, and Leanne, Julie, and Margaret are eager to build a snow person. Before heading outside, they talk with their mom, Katherine, about what their snow person will look like. Margaret shares that she wants to make Frosty with coal eyes, a carrot nose, and tree branches for arms. Julie points out that they do not have coal and that a carrot nose might get eaten by a rabbit. Margaret does not see how a rabbit could reach the snow person's carrot nose and still thinks that a carrot nose is a good idea. There is also a disagreement about what materials to use for the eyes: bottle caps or stones. Additionally, each girl has a different idea for the type of snow person she would like to make. Leanne is interested in making an alien, and Julie wants to make Bert, the chimney sweep from *Mary Poppins*. Katherine helps her daughters take time to listen to one another, respect different ideas, and negotiate a collaborative solution. Is it possible to make an alien Bert with a carrot nose? Each girl gathers materials, bundles up in snow gear, and heads out the door.

The snow is the perfect consistency. Julie packs a big hunk of snow in her hands, creating a snowball. Margaret and Leanne join her in rolling the ball in different directions, being careful to keep the ball from contacting the ground so it doesn't pick up gravel, dirt, and twigs. The girls pack the snow as the ball increases in size. Next Leanne rolls a snowball into a head. The girls flatten the top of the large bottom ball to provide stability for the snowball head. As they position the head on top of the body, Julie suggests that they work together to create a family of snow people. Their problem of identifying one snow character that they all agree on is solved. Besides, working together is more fun, and each girl's imagination is honored. The girls collaborate in making three snow people, each one adorned with appropriate accessories. Margaret runs inside the house to get a carrot and comes back breathless. "We didn't have any carrots, but I found this orange funnel that will work perfectly. I'm going to call my snow person Honker." The girls wrap scarves around the necks of their new snow friends to keep them warm.

Nature has the wonderful capacity to engage children's senses. Natural loose parts help children enter the realm of creativity and learn to preserve the future of the natural environments that surround us.

Part 4
Engagement

Focus

Scientists

Once you have commitment,
you need the discipline and
hard work to get you there.
—HAILE GEBRSELASSIE

Productivity

Solitude

Children are meaning-makers, and they play an active role in the acquisition of knowledge. For children, learning is dynamic, engaging, and social. They need to be actively engaged and interested to apply higher-order creative-thinking skills. Children are most engaged when they take an active role in constructing meaning, not when adults provide them with the information and expect them to memorize it. By encouraging children to meet challenges creatively, collaborate, and apply critical-thinking skills to real-world, unpredictable situations inside and outside of home and school, we prepare them for future college, career, and citizenship success.

Engagement, as defined in this chapter, is how children integrate and apply their social, emotional, physical, and cognitive capacities as they interact with the environment in both developmentally and contextually appropriate ways. Think of a time when you have immersed yourself wholeheartedly into an activity. You feel so engaged and are overcome by emotion and an intense need to complete the task. You know that you are learning and are interested in exploring more about the topic. You spend days testing new ideas until you gain a deep understanding. For example, Miriam is an amateur metalsmith and enjoys using the torch to fuse and move metal. She spent days figuring out how to create sculptural jewelry. She read, she experimented, and she talked to other jewelers. Miriam was not going to give up until she figured out the process and achieved the results she desired. The same happens when children are engaged in playing with loose parts. They explore, research, investigate, test new ideas, and ask questions. They are fully committed to the learning process, and they do not need adult praise or a reward. They know that their own accomplishment and discoveries are the best rewards.

Engagement is the interrelation of behavior, cognition, and emotion, giving us a more comprehensive way of looking at children's involvement. Children who are fully engaged are intrinsically motivated by curiosity, interest, and enjoyment and are likely to achieve their own intellectual goals. They are able to demonstrate self-control, concentration, productivity, working memory, deferred gratification, cognitive flexibility, and productivity (Jablon and Wilkinson 2006). Engagement leads to more profound learning and is the key to living a more intellectual life. Because of the open-ended nature of loose parts, they engage children in sustained investigations. When you observe children rolling balls of different sizes and materials down a ramp, you notice their facial expressions as they realize that the ball they thought would roll faster took longer. They encounter a new idea that challenges their ideas and understanding of how things function. This simple act engages them in testing different inclines and rolling the balls with a variety of speeds. They ask questions, change their hypothesis, and do not stop until they reach a conclusion. They are fully engaged in the activity. Psychologist Mihaly Csikszentmihalyi describes children in this state as being in the "flow." He describes being in the flow as that sense of effortless action people feel in moments that stand out as the best in their lives. That moment is also referred to as "being in the zone" or reaching full artistic rapture (Csikszentmihalyi 1997). When children are fully engaged, they feel that they are part of something larger, and they know that what they are doing is worth doing for its own sake, without the need for an external reward.

In her book *Engaging Children: Igniting Drive for Deeper Learning K–8*, Ellin Oliver Keene (2018, 62–63) defines the following four pillars of engagement:

1. **Intellectual urgency**: The feeling of "I have to know more" presents when children are intrigued by a conflict and search for solutions. Families and educators can promote intellectual urgency by giving children loose parts that challenge their thinking and engage their curiosity. For example, tin cans of different sizes combined with wooden blocks can challenge children's construction ability.

2. **Emotional resonance**: Children learn and are able to describe what they have learned when a strong emotion is attached to the experience. Take photographs of children's work and share the photographs with them. Give children an opportunity to describe how they felt as they created a work of art using natural materials such as leaves, pine cones, liquid amber, and other beautiful pods from nature.

3. **Perspective bending**: Children notice how others' knowledge, ideas, interests, and emotions affect their own. They are particularly interested in how their own beliefs and ideas affect others. Share your ideas with children and invite them to share theirs. Create opportunities for children to work with others and discuss why their collaborative work is so important. This can be done by planning an outing to a park, where children can explore different containers and sifters in the sandbox.

4. **The aesthetic world**: When children are engaged, they can describe when something beautiful, exciting, and aesthetically pleasing has affected them. Read books to children with beautiful illustrations, show them works of art by known artists, or take walks in your community and admire the beauty of nature. Give children bottle caps, glass beads, colorful felt balls, and natural

materials with which to create transient works of art. This is art that is not glued or permanent so it can be changed and revisited.

Children develop certain skills when they are engaged in explorations. In this chapter, we will unpack some of these skills in more detail.

Opportunities and Possibilities to Support Engagement

- Offer children tools and materials that support their ideas and interests.
- Create spaces where children can spend time designing, exploring, and testing their ideas.
- Slow down and take the time to play and engage in pleasurable exploration.
- Remember that boredom is the beginning of creativity; step back to give children the opportunity to discover their interests.
- Resist the temptation to hover over children, as they need space and time to concentrate and fully engage in exploration. Offer help only when asked.
- Have flexibility in daily schedules, because children need time to play, explore, and rest.
- Encourage solitude, which is one of the ways children enter into the realm of creativity. We all need time to reflect.

CHAPTER 10

Focus and Concentration

A popular misconception is that young children have short attention spans; however, when we observe them as they play, we see that they can focus for long periods of time. Children's curiosity is engaged as they watch water beads grow when they absorb water and shrink when they are left out of the water. Children are fully present and focused on finding answers and creating different ways to use the water beads. When adults take the time to observe this type of play, they can start identifying what children already know. They may ask questions such as, "What do you already know? What do you wonder about? What do you want to learn?" This strategy lets children know that their knowledge and interest is valued and respected. Children will focus and concentrate when they are engaged in explorations that are intriguing to them. Observe children investigating items that sink or float: they test, hypothesize, and take time to analyze the reasons why one item sinks and the other floats. Their focus and concentration are strengthened as their curiosity takes over.

Connection Captivation

It didn't surprise me to see the plastic golf balls joined with pipe cleaners. Harrison quietly sat on the kitchen floor and persisted in the task of inserting pipe cleaners in and out of golf ball holes to attach the balls together. Recently Harrison has been completely absorbed in connecting things. He spends time hooking train tracks and trains together. He has been attaching things together and tying things up. He connected pieces of PVC pipes and fittings to make a maze for water to run through. Last week Harrison was determined to secure two bamboo poles together with zip ties. He watched his hands intently as he secured each tie. Finally, after seventeen ties, he declared that the poles were stuck together.  He wrapped string back and forth between the side railings on the front porch, creating a trap to catch a giant. It's hard to distract him from his new interest. His intense concentration, focus, and perseverance will serve him well in the future to achieve goals, study, and work.

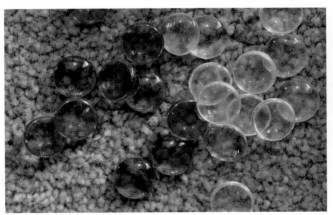

Candy box inserts are perfect containers for sorting gems.

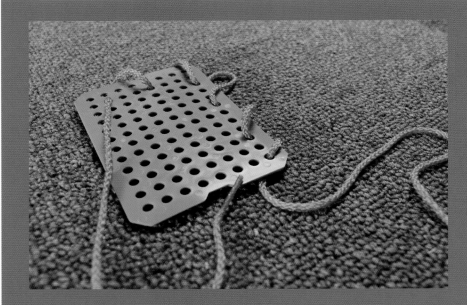

Joy and Frank have a knack for finding intriguing objects. One of their finds includes rectangular plastic templates with holes that are perfect for lacing. Charlotte has mastered threading pipe cleaners through plastic golf balls and is ready for a larger challenge. She focuses intently as she threads the cord in and out of the holes. She uses tremendous concentration as her eyes and hands coordinate visual information with her motor movements.

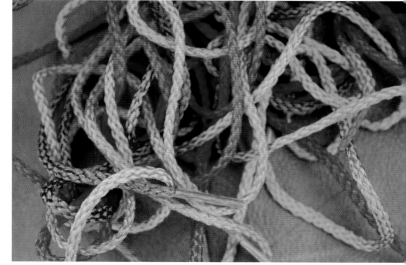

CHAPTER 11

Children as Scientists

Children are natural explorers and scientists and have remarkable capacities to gather, organize, and manipulate data. Children are capable of formulating and testing hypotheses, analyzing their findings, making corrections, and testing them again. Preschoolers have the ability to connect cause-and-effect relationships in the world and discern that these connections are governed by fundamental laws rather than by mysterious forces (Gopnik et al. 2001). Research like this has shown that children are capable of abstract thinking, proving that young children are more sophisticated in their explorations and reasoning than we give them credit for. The abilities to discern causal relationships and to think in abstract terms are important steps in children's development and will support them in their future academic pursuits.

Children need to play. In play children experiment with different patterns of repetition and immerse themselves in the enjoyment of learning. Play gives children the opportunity to experiment and test their ideas, to explore new possibilities, and to understand the consequences of their actions and decisions. As children engage in pretend play, they can imagine who they will be and what role they will play in the future. This prepares them to expect the unexpected and to accept change more readily. As you plan your weekly schedules, consider adding time for children to engage in open-ended play. Avoid rushing to the next activity and just step back and relax. Trust that children have deep knowledge and enjoy generating and exploring wonderful ideas. Hypothesizing and generating wonderful ideas is an active process that begins with the child's curiosity and is expanded by asking questions that interest them. Children are seekers of knowledge and apply scientific inquiry into their explorations. Step back and quiet your desire to intervene and teach them a lesson. Oftentimes when adults interrupt play, we take away children's focus and interest in scientific inquiry. The more they engage in loose parts play, the more they feel the joy of exploration and scientific inquiry that leads to an active search for knowledge. Loose parts play stimulates children's curiosity and builds science-related skills. Loose parts allow them to make decisions, test and revisit their ideas, and complete tasks. The concentration needed for a child to complete a task is self-motivated.

Scientist in the Making

Eddie, Chelsey's dad, reports that Chelsey is captivated by textures. Ever since she was an infant, she has loved to touch and stroke materials like the silky edge of her favorite blanket and the plush, velvety throw blanket where she likes to lie down. While visiting her grandparents in their new home, Chelsey takes a midday nap. Eddie takes advantage of the quiet time by setting up an

array of rich textures for Chelsey to investigate when she wakes. Chelsey comes downstairs to discover Eddie sitting on the carpeted floor next to an inviting selection of unfamiliar objects. Chelsey cautiously approaches the materials, grasps a silk scarf, and places it to her lips. She extends the scarf toward Eddie, showing him her new find. Chelsey  continues to pick up scarves one at a time as if to make certain that they all are silky. Eddie pulls a scarf through a cardboard ring and holds up the scarf's tip for Chelsey to grasp. She grips the scarf's end and begins to gently tug until the scarf slips through the ring. She smiles with satisfaction at her sense of accomplishment. Chelsey's inclinations reflect those of a scientist; she is observant, curious, and tests new ideas.

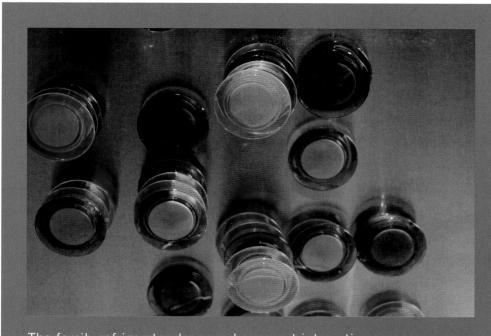

The family refrigerator door can be a great interactive canvas. Josh stacks circular magnetic disks on top of each other so that they project outward from the refrigerator door. He discovers that the magnet stack sways back and forth and in a circular motion as he places a magnet just above the stack. His actions control the magnets' movements.

CHAPTER 12

Productive Agency

When children are able to make meaningful decisions and choices about situations that directly affect them, they become agents in making a change. This is known as *agency*, a skill that children need to develop a sense of well-being and a strong identity. Agency involves being responsible, aware, motivated, and engaged. When children have a sense of agency, they actively and willingly participate to make meaningful changes to better their family, community, and world.

Harvard psychology professor Jerome Bruner expresses the importance of cultural agency in his book *The Culture of Education*: "Culture shapes minds, that it provides us with the toolkit by which we construct not only our worlds but our very conceptions of our selves and our powers" (1996, x). When families share their histories and traditions with children, they are providing children with a conceptual system that helps them organize their world. Children can then extrapolate their history, and in the future, they may begin to see themselves as agents who have a history and the capacity to create a positive future. Having a positive belief in oneself as an agent of change helps a child develop aspirations, confidence, and optimism.

Agency involves not only the capacity to initiate a change, but also the capacity to see it through to completion. This requires children to be flexible and have ways to deal with success as well as failure. Loose parts give children multiple opportunities to test ideas, explore different outcomes, and come up with diverse solutions. Balancing tubes one on top of the other engages children in identifying what may create a problem and generating, testing, and evaluating alternative solutions. During loose parts play, children's sense of agency propels them forward to continue to explore until they are satisfied with the outcome. Children can develop a sense of agency and independence when they are given time with other children and adults who build upon their learning. When we give children our focused attention, we can observe and find the moment to ask inquiry questions, which can scaffold learning. Deep learning occurs when children struggle instead of being given the answers, and recognizing this gives us the understanding that it may take longer for children to solve a problem and to develop the patience needed to facilitate the process. One of the most important features of all in children's play is their ability to imagine and to manipulate and organize loose parts in order to respond to those creative thoughts. When a sense of agency is present, children stay focused and engage their intellectual curiosity.

Chair-Back Canvas

Strong winds blew the thick, gray smoke and ash from the Northern California wildfires into the Sacramento Valley. The smoke persisted for many days in a row, creating unsafe air quality and prohibiting outdoor play. Restless from having to stay inside, Coryne turned a dining room chair back into her canvas for weaving. She sifted through the basket of fabric strips, stroking the various textures: rough burlap, fuzzy corduroy, and sticky carpet backing. She rubbed the smooth, silky satin against her cheek. At first she draped fabric strips over the chair's wooden slats, followed by twisting and weaving the strips in and out, up and down. Her actions shifted to her newly acquired skill of knot tying. Over and over again, she wrapped fabric around

the chair legs and secured each strip with her over, under, pull strategy of tying knots. Her work was a true demonstration of productivity and persistence as she initiated a creative idea and followed it through to completion.

Cassidy scooped birdseed into varying sizes of measuring cups and watched intently as she poured the birdseed over her outstretched fingers and then from one cup to another. She is learning about her agency in her control over her own actions and her ability to learn for herself the concepts of volume, quantity, trajectory, full, and empty.

CHAPTER 13

The Power of Solitude

Oh how we look for those quiet moments when we can just sit outdoors and reflect on our lives! Restorative power comes from those moments of solitude. Experiencing solitude helps us learn new ways of doing things, think creatively, and deal with emotions. These powerful moments of solitude can help us self-regulate, develop empathy, and improve social skills. Yet we have become a society always on the move. We expect children to be constantly engaged and involved in activities and play. When we see them quietly sit to the side, we may label them as shy. When children play in solitude, they are engaged in abstract thinking. They are taking the time to ponder a new idea, understand a new process, or simply reflect on when they will be ready to engage in play with other children.

Miriam's youngest daughter was one who sought solitude. Many adults labeled her shy and often pushed her to do things that were not comfortable for her. As an adult, she has shared with Miriam that when people thought she was shy, she was only observing and deciding what made her feel safe, reflecting on what she wanted to do. Today she is observant, reflective, and sensitive to her own emotions and supportive of other people. She is insightful and can easily identify what people need.

Renowned neuroscientist Dr. Bruce Perry argues that when children spend time in solo play, they are taking images, ideas, and concepts from their own minds and reorganizing them in ways that are meaningful to them.

In solitude children create hopes, wishes, and desires, and they dream of their future possibilities. Children need solitude and time away from constant stimulation so they can gain deeper knowledge and perspective as they play and learn (Perry 2016).

Boredom is a valuable process; through boredom children ponder and plan to creatively engage in play. As Miriam recounts, "When my children were little, they would sometimes complain about being bored. My standard response, which I am positive they hated, was, 'Good. Boredom is the beginning of creativity.' I would then guide them to find something that interested them. Soon they would be involved in a play exploration that engaged them."

Avoid jumping too soon to entertain children. Instead give them the time to be bored. Through boredom children's internal worlds come alive. This important process develops when children have moments of solitude when they can disconnect from outside stimulation and the incessant hovering of adults who think children need to be constantly entertained. When children are not made to be continually involved in daily activities, they will become more internally focused, and their creativity will take over. They will create toys, enchanting small worlds, and power structures from loose parts. They can become actors in a play, a rock can become a microphone, and blocks can be turned into a stage. The possibilities are endless.

Jeweled Towers

The stairwell windowsill in Heidi's house is a perfect spot if you want to be all by yourself. You can sit up on the extra-wide ledge to clip together craft sticks and clothespins, construct a sponge tower, thread shoelaces through beads, fold paper scraps, transform yarn into designs, or do nothing at all. On snowy nights, Marina likes to wrap a cozy blanket around herself and look out the window as large snowflakes drift down under the streetlight until the whole world turns white. Sometimes when she needs quiet time, Marina brings her treasure box to the windowsill and creates her own stories with things from her cherished box: small pieces of felt, buttons, broken earrings, keys, string, twist ties, and corks. Today a special surprise on the sill awaits Marina: a basket of colorful reusable ice cubes and small tongs. She finds delight in quietly building "jeweled" ice cube towers and walls as the sun illuminates the cubes and casts colorful images on the sill.

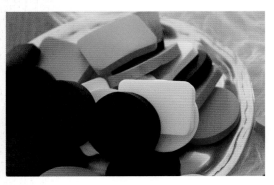
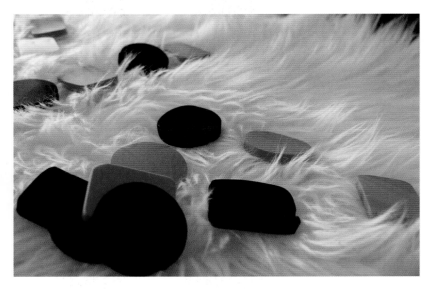

Serving cones made from bamboo plant leaves are used in Minhee's home for holding a variety of food, including fruit, snacks, and other finger foods. Today Minhee has her own quiet time as her younger sister takes a midday nap. She pretends that the glass stones are candy. Each cone is filled with candy and placed in her makeshift tamaki cone display.

Part 5
Risk

Physical Risks

Risk-Taking

Intellectual Risks

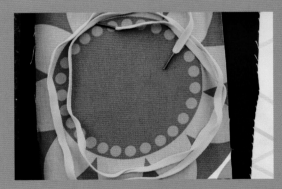

Social-Emotional Risks

It shouldn't surprise us that preschoolers are capable of boundless intellectual sophistication. The real surprise is that we subject them to testing and performance standards that often highlight the very dullest parts of their special minds.

—ERIKA CHRISTAKIS

When we think of risk, images of skydiving and rock climbing come to mind. These are activities in which one wrong move can mean serious injury or death. However, risk does not need to involve danger; it only needs to involve uncertainty or the illusion of risk.

We all remember the thrill of jumping from a high place (or what we thought was a high place), swinging on a rope, using a hammer or a screwdriver, roasting a marshmallow over the campfire, or playing hide-and-seek. The excitement and thrill of risk-taking and going on adventures is a memorable part of childhood because it combines the joy of freedom and just the right measure of fear to produce an exhilarating experience.

Children have a natural propensity for risk-taking, and research shows that taking risks is essential for optimal development and learning. Play involves a certain amount of innate risk-taking, so safety does need to be considered. Unfortunately, out of our fear we are creating environments that are "too safe." Overly safe environments present a different kind of danger for children. In his book *No Fear: Growing Up in a Risk Averse Society*, Tim Gill argues that growing up in a society that doesn't allow for risk means that children are not able to properly assess their own safety. As a result, many children become timid and reluctant to engage in play, or they may have difficulty reading situations they face, which leads them to take risks that can land them in trouble. Life is full of risks and challenges, and if we want to create a generation of children who can be successful in managing the not-yet-created work of the future, we need to provide them with opportunities to take risks (Gill 2007).

As a mother and early childhood educator, Miriam has memories of fear and concern as she watched her young daughters hanging upside down from a tree or hammering nails on a tree stump. She had to assess her "safety compass" and weigh the benefit of the play against the risk they were taking. With guidance and support from her mentors, who helped her assess her own fear and how to manage it, Miriam learned to give her daughters the opportunity to take risks. She carefully watched them as they tested their capacities. Miriam soon came to the understanding that as long as children are trusted to take risks and major hazards are controlled, they develop the ability to weigh risks on their own. This new knowledge helped shift the way Miriam looked at risk-taking. She learned to take care of the hazard and allow for the risk. She began to trust her daughters' abilities to know their limits and began to look at the environment in a way that mitigated possible hazards while providing opportunities to engage in challenging "real" play. Real play means taking risks, which benefits children in many ways:

- fostering physical, social, and cognitive development
- allowing children to face the risk of making mistakes and deal with the consequences
- encouraging children to embrace life with joy and enthusiasm instead of fear
- supporting risk-assessment development, which allows children to match their skills with the demands of the environment
- helping children gain awareness of genuine danger and avoid getting into trouble
- building agency and resiliency
- aiding children in gaining a sense of power and control over their world
- providing opportunities to practice independent thinking and reflection
- promoting social interactions and collaborative play

Many children today spend too much time indoors watching television, playing video games, or engaging in adult-led activities. Opportunities to participate in self-initiated play are often limited. As a result of cultural, social, and economic factors, children's lives have become more restricted. Opportunities to explore their neighborhoods on their own or to walk in the woods unaccompanied have diminished considerably. Shifting our perception of risk-taking and incorporating loose parts play, especially large loose parts outdoor play, can go a long way in supporting children's development of their own risk compass.

Opportunities and Possibilities to Support Risk-Taking

- Set up an environment where the focus is on learning rather than getting the right answers. Because intellectual risk-taking can be threatening, children need an environment where they feel safe to make mistakes and test their ideas and hypotheses.
- Allow children to make mistakes and find alternate solutions. Give them time to test their ideas and hypotheses. When children play with blocks, they build and build until they are satisfied with their structure. In moments when frustration may arise, help children learn to take a step back, regroup, and then come back to the play. The more confident they feel in controlling their emotions, the more flexible they become in their thinking.
- Joke, laugh, and be joyful along with the children. When they learn that life does not always have to be so serious, they can take the difficult times in stride, and challenging moments pass more easily.

- Step back and give children the opportunity to play and make choices. Avoid interfering, and only offer help when asked. Trusting children builds their self-confidence and positive beliefs about their abilities. They will be more willing to take on leadership roles and guide others in creating innovative projects.

- Provide various loose parts that allow children to gain control over their play instead of purchasing toys that are useless once the child masters them.

- Value error correction and progress, not perfection. Comment on how children are taking a risk and challenging themselves. Encourage them to continue to test their ideas and challenge each other.

- Let them learn from their failures instead of protecting them from experiencing failure. When children skin their knees climbing a rock wall but keep on climbing to reach the top, they are reassured that they can overcome obstacles quickly. This knowledge translates well to other risky life decisions presented in childhood.

- Allow children to discover their own success. They need to learn the excitement that comes from achieving a goal. Having victories in play helps children move past failure and frustration and gives them the perseverance to try and try again, even when they may feel uncomfortable or think the task is too hard.

- Embrace a philosophy of resilience. Trust in children's ability to recover and learn from adverse outcomes.

CHAPTER 14

Learning about Risk-Taking Capacities

Begin by reflecting on your own safety compass. Go back to your play memories and revisit the risks you took as a child. What did you learn from these experiences? Did you value the process and the learning? Now consider how you will create spaces that provide children the opportunity to develop their play memories. Balance the risk with the benefit. What will your children learn as they build with small loose parts? Can we control the fear of a choking hazard and allow for the learning to take place? What spaces can you modify within your living environment to enable children to engage in play? For example, can you replace the content of some of the bottom kitchen cabinets with plastic, metal, and wood containers that can be used in play and exploration?

Playing in the Kitchen

While her father is cooking, Nichole takes out pots and proceeds to match the different-size lids to the pots. After a while, she notices that her father is using different wooden spoons to stir the food he is cooking, and she proceeds to imitate him. Nichole's father invites her to step on a stool, and under direct supervision, he allows her to help him cook. Nichole is trusted because she has demonstrated her capacity to handle risks in the kitchen. Her parents have learned to provide a space to explore rather than block her out of the kitchen for safety reasons. Nichole has also learned to enter the area only in the company of caring adults. She has developed a strong safety compass and uses it successfully.

During a visit to Momo's house, Trinity discovers materials in the kitchen that she has not seen on previous visits. At first she holds back and cautiously observes. After having time to assess, she risks a closer look and touches the materials. She fills her pot with bottle caps and begins to stir.

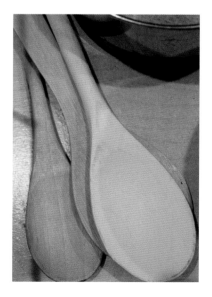

The thrill of watching a ball rolling down cove molding placed in the staircase can be exhilarating. Children naturally seek play that is challenging and a bit scary. The quivering feeling of butterflies in their belly when they follow the ball down the stairs helps them assess their risk capacities.

CHAPTER 15

Physical Risks

Do you have memories of rolling downhill, chasing other children, bouncing on trampolines, walking across wooden planks, swinging high, coming down headfirst on the slide, wrestling, having pillow fights, and fencing with branches or wooden dowels? This type of play requires taking physical risks and engaging in rigorous kinds of behaviors that are part of rough-and-tumble play. Roughhousing is dynamic, spontaneous, and full of joy. It is free from time commitments or daily expectations. It promotes physical fitness, helps children relax, and supports overall development and well-being. Unfortunately adults' perceptions of rough-and-tumble play as an aggressive activity have prevented many children from experiencing it. When we take a closer look at the importance of roughhousing, we begin to see its value.

In the book *The Art of Roughhousing: Good Old-Fashioned Horseplay and Why Every Kid Needs It*, Dr. Anthony DeBenedet and Dr. Lawrence Cohen (2010, 11) state, "Most important, roughhousing is *rowdy*, but not dangerous. With safety in mind, roughhousing releases the creative life force within each person, pushing us out of our inhibitions and inflexibilities." Large-muscle physical play activates many parts of the body and brain. Sergio Pellis, a researcher at the University of Lethbridge, Alberta, Canada, argues that rough-and-tumble play supports new neuronal connections in the frontal cortex and hippocampus regions of the brain. These are the parts of the brain responsible for memory, learning, language, logic, and high executive functions (Pellis, Pellis, and Bell 2010). Roughhousing also activates the amygdalae, which process emotions, and the cerebellum, which handles complex motor skills. In his book *Affective Neuroscience: The Foundations of Human and Animal Emotions*, Dr. Jaak Panksepp (2014) connects physical play to learning. He argues that during rough-and-tumble play, children begin to behave in flexible, creative, and emphatic ways. Other important aspects of physical play include the opportunity to make mistakes without fear of repercussion, as well as the ability to change rules and test new ideas.

The Swashbuckling Challenge

On a sunny day, Marcel, Henry, and their father, Lance, go to the park to play with cardboard tubes that were donated by a printing shop. They look through the tubes, stand next to the tubes to measure their height, balance them, and use them to reach the basketball hoop. As their play continues, the tubes become baseball bats, and as Henry swings, he hits Marcel and a game of swashbuckling begins. Dad joins in, and their laughter is contagious. They practice moving back and forth and touching each other with the tubes. Rules are negotiated, and they agree that if one of them says to stop, the other will stop. This game goes on for a while, and once they all are tired, they say stop and the game ends. Using soft cardboard tubes is a safe way to engage in

roughhousing. It helps children negotiate and learn about one another's body language. Not only did Marcel and Henry undertake substantial physical challenges, but they also developed the ability to take social and emotional risks.

There is a certain level of risk when you throw a ball up into the air and attempt to catch it. All your physical capacities come into play. You need to propel the ball by using your large muscles, carefully track it as it comes down, and allow your reflexes to respond as you extend your hand to catch it. Catching a ball can become a more significant challenge when using milk containers that have been turned into catching tools.

CHAPTER 16
Social-Emotional Risks

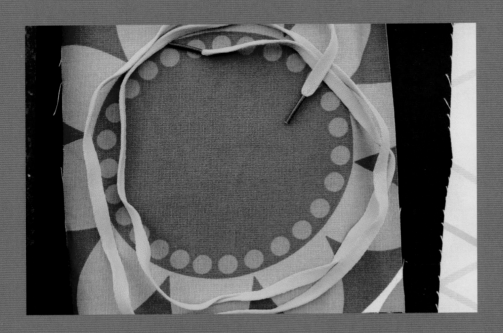

Remember a time when you worked for days to complete a project. You probably spent time thinking about it, planning it, and executing your idea. Then it was time to take an emotional risk and share your work with others. You did not know if they were going to like it, give you suggestions on what to change, or criticize your work. What you did know is that you had worked hard and were happy with your creation. Think about a time when you met a new group of people. You had to take a social risk and join them in conversation. Both emotional and social risks are a reality of daily life.

Play offers multiple opportunities to take both social and emotional risks, which help children gain control of their environment, develop agency, and strengthen their self-identity. When children play with loose parts, they gain the freedom to act and make choices. They also work collaboratively to solve problems. In play children use independence-enhancing skills that allow them to develop autonomy and gain the experience and confidence needed to become fully functioning adults. Play offers children the opportunity to figure out the rules, negotiate, and learn to argue and communicate effectively. They learn to read and interpret one another's body language and know when to stop or continue the play.

Loose parts play also allows children to process their feelings and emotions safely.

A group of children wearing scarves as capes begin a game of chase. They pretend to fly, and each has superpowers. Jessica joins in the game, and Peter catches her. She stops, and in a teary voice says, "Stop. That is not fair." Peter sees her eyes and exclaims, "I don't want to make you cry. We don't need to chase each other." Peter and Jessica spend time roughhousing with peers and family members. They have learned to read each other's body language and clues. They have also learned to respond to each other's needs and have been able to build empathy to understand other people's perspectives. Their play shifts to using water bottles to spray each other. Before they start, they make the rules. They decide that they can spray each other on the face but that they will stay off the patio because they don't want to get the furniture wet. Listening to the negotiations reminds us of how capable and competent they are in assessing each other's feelings and respecting the ideas presented in the discussion.

A Colorful Mural

Aaron uses colorful bottle caps to create a mural on the living room floor. After lunch his friend Jason comes over to spend the afternoon and Aaron goes back to his creation. Jason asks Aaron to go outside to play ball, but Aaron ignores him and continues to work on his mural. Jason goes to the floor and starts to take bottle caps away from Aaron's design. Aaron turns around and tells Jason in a loud voice, "No, I am working with those caps." Jason looks at Aaron and realizes that he is not angry; he is protecting his work. He asks Aaron, "Can  help?" Aaron nods and moves to make space for Jason. After a while, they go outside to play ball for the rest of the afternoon.

Aaron's parents recognize that Aaron raising his voice is a protective urge and not an aggressive reaction. They know that the boys are taking an emotional risk as they find a space to play with each other. They are also validating that the boys have the right to own and be responsible for the things they love and the right to protect their hard work. When children associate a positive feeling with an emotion, they will be less likely to yell in the future. Aaron will also learn that there are different ways to express his feelings that can lead to a more successful outcome. With adult guidance, both Jason and Aaron learned to respond to each other's needs in respectful and supportive ways.

What is more enjoyable, wrapping the climbing structure in tape, or taking down the tape? Marcel and Henry seem to enjoy the entire process thoroughly. They are relaxed, and their laughter shows us how well they get along with each other and how emotionally at peace they are as they enter the flow of play and creativity.

SOCIAL-EMOTIONAL RISKS **175**

CHAPTER 17

Intellectual Risks

Asking questions, sharing ideas with other people, and learning new things are all forms of intellectual risk-taking because they place the learner at risk of making mistakes or appearing less competent than others. Intellectual risk-taking is an adaptive behavior, as the benefits of engaging in this type of risk-taking far outweigh the consequences (Beghetto 2009). Engaging in intellectual risk-taking requires children to confront the fear, anxiety, and uncertainty of success and acceptance. When children experience intellectual risk, they are building skills of negotiation, such as reaching consensus and making informed decisions. At three years of age, Diego has tremendous knowledge about trains and how they work. He knows the name of every *Thomas the Tank Engine* character and can tell you about them with great confidence. When children feel competent about a subject, they will be more likely to ask questions, engage in a discussion, and explore the possibility of multiple outcomes.

Intellectual risk-taking connects to a wide range of skills needed to function beyond the twenty-first century. The Partnership for 21st Century Learning has identified thinking, creative, and innovative skills that children will need to be productive in the unknown workforce of the future (2019). One of the important traits they identified is the understanding that creativity and innovation is a long-term cyclical process requiring adaptability, flexibility, and knowledge. Before achieving success, mistakes are bound to happen; correcting them and continuing to explore new possibilities will lead children to view failure as an opportunity for learning. When children share ideas, they are forging their own identity as competent and capable explorers and learners. They are learning to challenge their thinking and taking a risk to add to their current knowledge and understanding of how the world functions. Intellectual risk-taking is also related to creativity and metacognition, the awareness and understanding of one's thought processes, which are both essential precursors to academic success. Even though there is no formal agreement on a single definition of creativity, research shows that intellectual risk-taking is frequently identified as an essential trait of creative people (Tyagi et al. 2017). Metacognitive knowledge includes knowing yourself as a learner and supports planning, comprehension, and the decision to use specific strategies to meet a goal. Metacognition gives children the ability to self-evaluate and assess whether an idea will work or what changes need to be made to make the idea work. When children have the opportunity to create, test, and present an innovative idea, they are learning that their concept may be received successfully or that it may encounter criticism that needs to be addressed. Either way they are taking a valuable intellectual risk.

How Far the Balls Roll

Juan, Ariana, and Leonard find a large wooden shelf in the backyard. They notice that the shelf can become a ramp and start to figure out how to prop it up to create different inclines. They roll a ball down the ramp to see how far it goes. They hypothesize and discuss their ideas, and they add rubber siding to extend the ramp. They spend the morning testing different inclines and a variety of balls to see how far they roll. They make a series of predictions and find different ways to test them. Juan suggests that they start recording their ideas. Ariana runs into the house and returns with paper and a pencil. The children start to discuss who will roll the balls and who will record the results. They carefully plan and execute their strategies. Leonard walks to the side of the house and returns with a yardstick, exclaiming, "Now we can really see how far they roll."

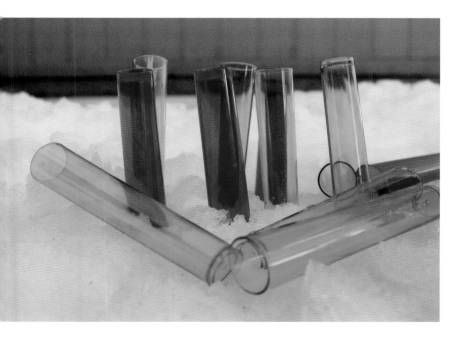

Balancing, defying gravity, and building tall structures using blocks challenge children's intellect in profound ways. They have to consider the multiple possibilities and challenges that the different shapes and sizes of blocks offer them.

Part 6
Innovative Thinking

Cycle of Innovation

Design Thinking

Inquisitiveness

Ambiguity

If a child is to keep alive his inborn sense of wonder . . . he needs the companionship of at least one adult who can share it, rediscovering with him the joy, excitement, and mystery of the world we live in. —RACHEL CARSON

Robotics, smart systems, 3-D printing, solar power, artificial intelligence, and biotechnology are just a few of the advances we currently use to tackle everyday problems. Concurrently with these incredible advances, we also have to address a variety of socioeconomic challenges, such as demographics, geopolitical issues, global warming, and supply-chain management, among others. With all these changes, we have learned to adapt our thinking and skills to adjust and meet the demands that come with change.

As the world continues to rapidly change, questions concerning the education of children surface: What skills, knowledge, and dispositions will they need to be successful in the twenty-first and even twenty-second century? What type of training will children need to develop these skills, knowledge, and dispositions? In 2016 the World Economic Forum (2016) published *The Future of Jobs: Employment, Skills, and Workforce Strategy for the Fourth Industrial Revolution.* In this comprehensive report, they identified the following top six skills people will need to function in the workforce of the future:

- innovation
- creativity
- critical thinking
- complex problem solving
- strategic thinking
- collaboration
- communication

All of these skills are essential to developing and bringing to life innovations that solve real problems and provide meaningful value. For children to acquire these skills, we need to rethink educational systems from the limiting academic-driven curriculum that currently exists to a more intellectual and creatively engaging process. Ingenuity, creativity, and innovative thinking are characteristics that make us human and drive our ability to solve problems. Children need to play and tinker to develop the innovative thinking needed in the future.

Loose parts play provides children with the opportunity to tinker, to be creative, and to come up with innovative solutions that promote change. Families and educators have the opportunity to help children develop many of the skills they need by providing play spaces that encourage innovation. Consider the idea of building forts; this is a fundamental and common experience in childhood. Many of us have fond memories of building forts for hiding, gathering with friends, or reading in a secluded space. The act of building forts using sheets, towels, fabrics, and crates is much like an engineering process. When children design the forts, they are using loose parts and transforming them into viable systems. They are creating make-believe spaces that allow them to be themselves. When children use loose parts, they are developing cognitive skills as they calculate the number of yards of fabric needed to cover a space. They experiment with tension and compression as they stretch the fabric over crates or furniture. They explore the structural integrity of their forts as they invent solutions to hold the materials in place. When children play with loose parts, they use their minds and imaginations to gain an understanding of spatial awareness and how things work. When we encourage children's inherent drive to play and to construct personal worlds and spaces, we foster their competency and confidence. These are essential skills to be an innovator. Tinkering with loose parts is valuable because it allows children's brains to enter a state of being that is not linear, driven, or goal oriented. Instead they develop the flexibility to explore different solutions to solve a problem. Loose parts play builds persistence and grit, which are the essential characteristics of great innovators.

Opportunities and Possibilities to Support Innovative Thinking

- Remember that when children are in the process of learning something new, they may experience a moment of discomfort. Give them the support to get through it without giving them answers.
- Practice asking a variety of questions that help children think innovatively.
- Ask creative questions that help children think divergently or come up with multiple possible answers.
- Ask critical questions that help them delve deeper into exploring a concept.
- Ask sensory questions that allow them to describe how an object looks or feels.
- Ask thought questions that help them predict what may happen or why things seem different.
- Ask historical questions that help them think of how things that happened in the past affect us today. For young children, it may be about things that happened just a few days ago.
- Ask futuristic questions that help them think of possibilities for the future.

- Ask Socratic questions that help them predict and analyze what may happen to an idea they have.
- Select a variety of loose parts and make them available for children to use throughout the day.
- Help children plan, gather, ideate, and execute their design.
- Encourage children to explore, investigate, and engage in loose parts play with other children.
- Learn to value a flexible learning process and focus on the development of intellectual learning instead of just academic learning.

CHAPTER 18

The Cycle of Innovation

Innovation promotes significant change that disrupts the status quo. By *disruption* we do not mean behaving negatively; instead we see disruption as the process of instigating meaningful change that leads to positive results. Disruption is about understanding that it is not what you study and learn but what interests you and makes you want to pursue further knowledge that matters. Innovators can create change through the inventive use of technology or promote equity through social innovation. The critical question that we need to ask ourselves as both educators and family members is how to cultivate the necessary skills and knowledge in young children for them to become future innovators. Allowing children to question, explore, investigate, and change will help them engage in disruption and innovation.

Creating momentum that enables children to follow an idea and pursue learning is also an essential part of innovation. This momentum sometimes may look like children are just following an idea without any particular structure. This is the time when adults can guide them to analyze their work, ask questions, and find strategies that can help assess what they need to integrate their ideas and make them come to fruition. Ask a child what tools they may need, how the devices will work, and how they can allow their project to follow an interesting direction. Innovative people do not take no for an answer. The cycle of innovation involves a continuing search for a possible solution and often begins anew when there is a disruption to that solution. Innovation requires passion, commitment, and adults who believe in the many ways children learn. In his book *Creating Innovators: The Making of Young People Who Will Change the World*, Tony Wagner writes, "Play, passion, and purpose have been every bit as important in their development, as was having parents who supported them in the pursuit of their passions and the influence of an outlier teacher or mentor who made a significant difference in their lives" (2012, 102). Loose parts engage children's passion to create and innovate as they pursue their ideas and interests. Through loose parts play, children will become the successful innovators and leaders of the future.

The Disappearing Spoons

Sebastian enjoys hiding items around the house. He is particularly fascinated with fitting loose parts into different small enclosures. At one point, all the spoons in the kitchen disappeared. The family was perplexed until they found them in the heater vent near the kitchen. This shows his interest in and the schema of insert-

ing. By recognizing it as a schema, his family was willing to provide other opportunities for him to continue to explore inserting. Because of his innovative thinking and interest in household items, his mother gave him a basket with colanders and wooden dowels, empty boxes of tissue and old spoons, and an old spice holder with tubes. She also gave him pipe cleaners to insert into corrugated plastic tiles. This helped Sebastian redirect his interest while continuing to make connections to science, engineering, and mathematical concepts by exploring ideas like how many dowels can fit into a hole, which tube is bigger, and complex counting and seriation strategies.

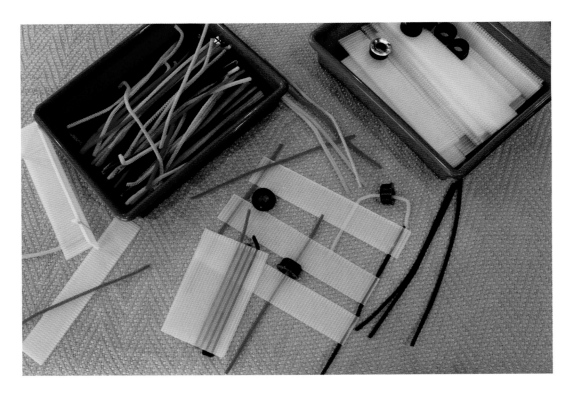

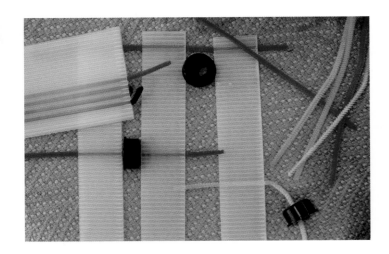

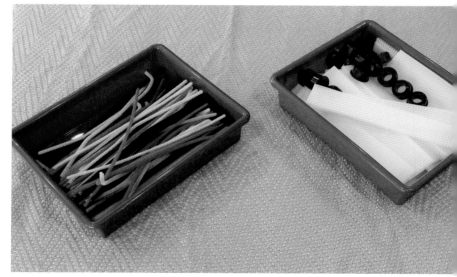

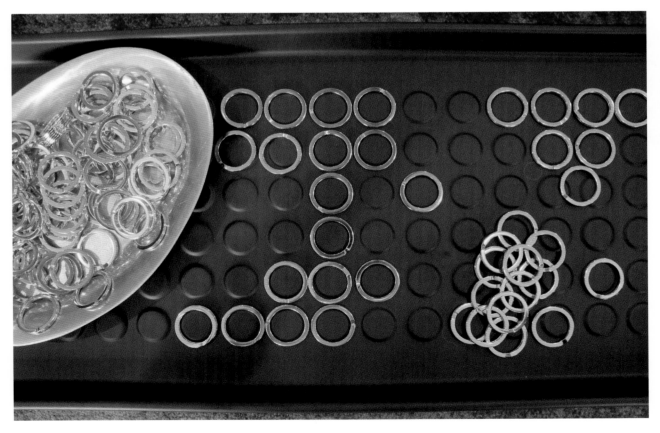

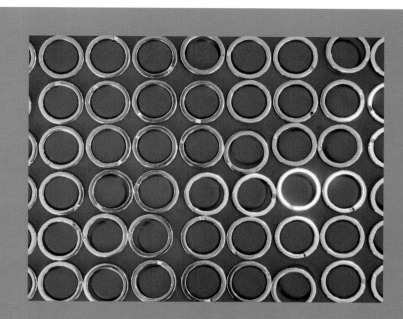

Sumaya is curious about what she can do with metal rings. She discovers that the rings fit perfectly around each raised circle of their shoe mat. The shoe mat is upcycled into her design canvas. She persists until every raised circle on the mat is surrounded by a ring. Through her play, she has created an innovative design with loose parts.

CHAPTER 19
Design Thinking

Defining how we work and our approach to solving complex business problems is a challenge in itself. Children today will someday be the leadership of the future. They will need to be able to reframe the way they approach challenges. Design thinking provides a process that allows children to think innovatively about devising solutions that are responsive to people's needs while also supporting their strengths. The first principle of design thinking is empathy, or listening, and observing with your heart. Empathy builds on the definition of "walking in someone else's shoes" and helps us understand others' reality so that we can meet the implicit demands of specific situations. Empathy pushes us to connect with people and opens our minds to opportunities and possibilities we might not have considered before. Loose parts play can engage children in analyzing and understanding different perspectives. The open-ended nature of the materials allows children to feel, construct, and understand the range of human emotions. This connection to human emotions is one of the important precursors to innovative and design thinking.

Design thinking is a collaborative process and stems from the idea that great minds are stronger together. When children work collaboratively to solve a problem, they challenge each other. Through interaction with other children, they learn to value multiple perspectives, thus increasing their ability to innovate and create change. Loose parts play provides children with opportunities to collaborate and negotiate with each other as they build, play, and solve problems. Children begin to challenge assumptions so that when they confront a problem, they approach it with an open mind and willingness to experiment and find different solutions. Loose parts encourage design thinking by embracing children's curiosity and helping them see beyond the object to appreciate its functionality and possibilities.

The Metal Tin Collection

Erik, Susan, and Jonathan love to play outdoors at their grandfather's house during their summer break. During a weeklong visit, they decide to build a structure with tin containers but can only find a few tins around the house. There are not enough for their plan. Grandfather takes the children around the neighborhood to ask neighbors to save metal tins for them. They place a large box in front of the house and check every day to see how many tins they have received. By the end of the week, they have enough tins to build tall structures. They discuss how tall they will build their structure and wonder how they are going to place tins on top of the tower when it is beyond their reach. Repeatedly the tins topple before they can stack them all on the tower. The children unknowingly use a design-thinking process to solve their problem. They begin by observing what happens when they attempt to stack the tins taller, and talk with one another about their experiences to gain an understanding of the issues involved. They identify that their arms are knocking into the tins and causing them to fall. Susan believes that they are not tall enough and that the grassy surface may be uneven. They generate ideas to solve their problem and look at alternatives. Erik suggests standing on a stool. Jonathan proposes that they hold up Erik, the youngest child, to put a tin on top. Susan believes that they may need to move their structure by a retaining wall so that they can stand on the wall. They test Jonathan's solution of holding up Erik to place the final tins on top. They persist and practice building with patience and enthusiasm. Refinements are made until finally all the tins are stacked in one tall tower. Their ability to arrive at innovative solutions is an essential skill to be successful in the future.

As Thomas plays with the wooden floor samples, he tells his dad that people can slip on smooth tiles and that textured tiles are hard to clean. He is aware of people's needs and knows that needs influence design. Thomas is demonstrating empathy and making clear connections between how people function and how that influences the way we build, create, and design items.

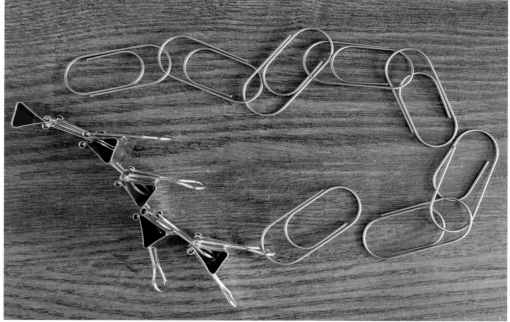

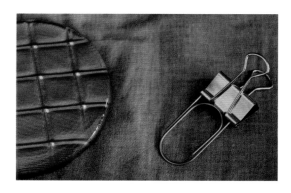

CHAPTER 20

Inquisitiveness and Curiosity

Children are curious, and most of us have probably been the subject of their constant "why" questions. Learning occurs as children wonder, explore, and question things that happen around them. Children are attracted to novelty and objects that offer multiple possibilities for exploration. As adults we marvel when we watch a child build a complex structure using blocks, miniature tree stumps, and tree cookies only to push it over and make it tumble. For them the purpose may be an interest in how things fall, the power they have over the materials, or just the sound the items make as they fall. What is important is that in this exploration, children are learning about cause and effect and their capacities over the materials. When children fill and dump sand or water into different containers, they are learning about mass and volume. Their curiosity and inquisitiveness lead them to continually explore and attempt to find answers to their millions of questions.

There are times when leaving questions without answers can engage children in explorations to find multiple answers for themselves. Children may be looking for specific answers, but they are also ready to engage in more in-depth investigation driven by their inquisitiveness. Socratic or inquiry questions are a great way to get children's creative juices flowing. Inquiry questions help children transition from looking for right or wrong answers to making comparisons, analyzing different solutions, entertaining new ideas, and formulating personal responses. Asking inquiry questions or essential questions focused on what children are interested in makes their thinking visible. Remember that questions need to have context or they may be too difficult for children to comprehend. For example, children living in an urban setting may not have the experience of being on a farm. Tailor questions to the current experiential knowledge of the children. Observe and listen to what they say in their play to give you the context to engage in the inquiry process. When children are given the opportunity to explore and satisfy their curiosity, they develop divergent and innovative thinking skills, which sustain motivation and engage their passion for in-depth learning. Inquisitiveness encourages children to continually generate new ideas, think up new solutions to complex problems, and grow as innovative thinkers.

Balancing Candlesticks

Sergio is balancing candleholders up and down the entry steps and is challenged by the variety of sizes. He attempts to place a larger-size candlestick on top of a slightly smaller one. The steps are also uneven, which adds an extra challenge to the exploration. His father approaches him and asks, "Sergio, I noticed that the candlestick you are placing on top keeps falling. What do you think is making that happen?" Sergio stops building and takes a closer look at the candlesticks. He realizes that the candlestick he had placed on top of the structure was bigger than the bottom one. Sergio then sits closer to the stairs and examines them. He exclaims, "The stairs are not straight, and this is bigger [pointing to the larger candlestick]. I am going to move it to another part

of the stair and use the bigger candlestick at the bottom." By asking an inquiry question, Sergio's father engaged him in deeper thinking and motivated him to explore other possibilities.

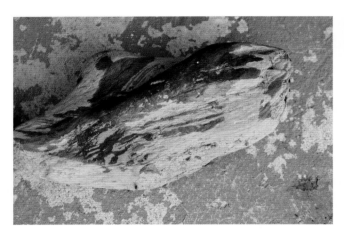

There is nothing quite as satisfying as watching the immediate transformation in appearance of items brushed with water. Trinity paints water on driftwood, changing the dry, dull wood to a rich, glossy brown. She continues her experimentation by stroking water on the house siding with different brushes.

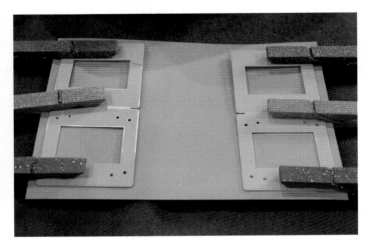

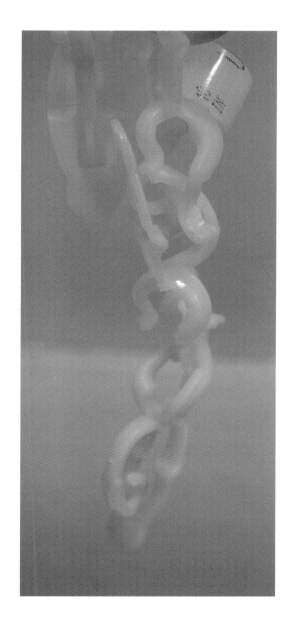

CHAPTER 21

Uncertainty and Ambiguity

In the twenty-first century, what you know is far less important than what you can do with that knowledge. Innovation exists in the world of ambiguity, where every situation involves uncertainty, and we need to be prepared to respond when unexpected things happen. The free-flowing process of innovation necessitates the existence of ambiguity and uncertainty before clarity. Innovation requires tolerance for uncertainty and ambiguity, patience, and understanding that not all questions will be answered immediately. However, ambiguity is a helpful tool that can help children pinpoint the challenges they are facing and dig deeper into the reason behind a problem. This process requires time. If we rush children through the uncertainty and ambiguity of the cycle of innovation, they will never advance in their ability to innovate and make essential contributions to themselves and the community they live in.

Innovation requires us to embrace the process instead of focusing on the final product. Loose parts play allows children to explore and learn to be flexible as they find answers to their questions. The open-ended nature of loose parts gives children the ability to try new perspectives, make changes, and start again when they want to. Children seem to instinctually understand that there are no right or wrong answers or ways to achieve their goals. They recognize that the process is more important than the outcome. When we observe children playing with blocks, we see that they want to build the structure because it's fun, not because they want to have a tower. Guiding children to tolerate the ambiguity of the innovative process and push through it to find answers will help them address the uncertainty of everyday events.

As educators we have come to believe that the fear of failure is what is holding children back in learning. As adults we spend too much time preventing children from failing. We are inundating them with remedial reading and writing programs. We are working hard at getting them ready for their next step in their education. We talk about incremental learning and argue that children need to know certain things before they can learn others. We want to make sure that specific outcomes are met, and we hold people accountable (including children) if they are not met because we have a tremendous fear of failure. However, our fear is different. We fear that if we continue in this linear path, we won't have future innovators that can change the world. Innovation requires us to create education that helps children think without a box, tolerate ambiguity and uncertainty, and push through difficult tasks to find answers to their questions. If we are to have future innovators, we must change our practices and learn to address our fear of failure and our uncertainties.

The Key Collection

Joey, a three-year-old, is sorting and classifying a collection of keys. Joleen, his five-year-old sister, comes over and shares a different way of arranging them by making a tyrannosaurus rex. This play leads to a critical conversation of differing perspectives as far as how to use the keys. Joey wants to copy his sister's idea because he admires her and follows her around, but he also wants to hold on to his own ideas. Joey may need support to understand that it is possible and acceptable to hold contradictory or opposite ideas and feelings in his mind at the same time. Curiosity gives children the opportunity to wonder and to play with ideas that are ambiguous or uncertain.

Water is scarce in the imaginative world created by Janelle and Tony. They come up with an innovative solution to sustain their kingdom with water for a long time. Their plan is to use water beads. They watch with intrigue as the beads become larger and larger when submerged in water. The beads are divided into cupcake holders so that Janelle and Tony may distribute them fairly to the kingdom's residents—quite a creative solution to a complicated problem.

Part 7
Creativity

Joy

Messiness

Engagement

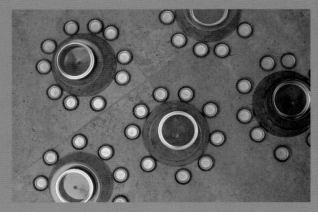
Curiosity

It is through feelings as well as through reason that we find our real creative power. It is through both that we connect with each other and create the complex, shifting worlds of human culture. —KEN ROBINSON

When we imagine creativity, we often think of creative geniuses like the artists and musicians Pablo Picasso, Leonardo da Vinci, and Wolfgang Amadeus Mozart. Many of us have been asked, "Are you creative?" and our answers may be based on the preconceived ideas of what we know about creativity. In his book *The Origins of Creativity*, Pulitzer Prize–winner Edward O. Wilson (2017) describes creativity as the "innate quest for originality" and argues that creativity is judged by the emotional responses it evokes. We have a preconception that creativity is something that people are born with and that it cannot be learned. We may have received messages in childhood imparting judgment of our creativity, thus making us see ourselves as uncreative. However, to nurture creativity in children, we must have a different understanding.

A more realistic and productive view is that creativity is the process of making new connections to old ideas, understanding the relationships between concepts, and taking what already exists and combining bits and pieces into something that has not been done before. We can reframe how we view creativity and start to see that nearly every person is born with some level of creativity and that the majority of innovative-thinking abilities are trainable. Dr. Barbara Kerr proposed that approximately 22 percent of the variance in creativity is influenced by genes. She made this discovery as she studied the difference in creative thinking in twins (2009). In the same study, Kerr discovered that some personality traits are common in creative people; for example, creative people seem to be less conforming and less concerned with how people perceive them. However, only through interactions with the environment are creative behaviors fully developed.

Current scientific studies on creativity have focused on the functioning of the brain during creative moments. They seek to understand how the brain reacts during moments of insightful thought. These studies showed that creative thinking involves making new connections between different regions of the brain, which happens when people engage in divergent thinking and encounter new experiences. In the book *Wired to Create: Unraveling the Mysteries of the Creative Mind*, authors Scott Barry Kaufman and Carolyn Gregoire (2015) describe how creative people engage in flexible thinking and thought processes that use various parts of their brains. These integrated thought processes include generating new ideas, expanding and fleshing out the ideas, critically reflecting, and considering the perspective of the audience. The creative process is not linear; creative people tend to engage in more than one exploration or interest concurrently and generate multiple ideas simultaneously. Mihaly Csikszentmihalyi (2013, 57), a renowned expert on creativity, summarizes, "If I had to express in one word what makes [creative people's] personalities different from others, it would be *complexity*. By this I mean that they show tendencies of thought and action that in most people are segregated. They contain contradictory extremes—instead of being an 'individual,' each of them is a 'multitude.'" He argues that the truly meaningful parts of being a human being are products of creativity and that during creative moments we are fully alive.

According to researcher Rex Jung (2014), creativity is the ability of the brain to use abductive reasoning and to solve adaptive problems in the environment in novel and useful ways. Abductive reasoning is hypothesis generation based on the best available evidence. It requires people to think in abstract and metaphorical terms. It also utilizes approximation, making inferences from the best available information. Approximation requires people to generate multiple "best guesses" before proposing an optimal and novel solution to a problem. This may present a challenge in young children, but with practice, they can develop the capacity to use inference to devise best guesses and test their creative hypotheses. Humanistic psychologist Carl Rogers argued that for the creative thinking process to emerge, there needs to be an openness to new experiences. Actions to support such openness include creating conditions that are less restrictive and linear and displaying tolerance for ambiguity where ambiguity exists (C. Rogers 1954). To support children's creativity, as adults we have to keep wondering and allow our curiosity to guide our own learning. We need to create conditions that are devoid of judgment and instead demonstrate unconditional acceptance of children's explorations. We want to provide children with space and environments where they can derive enjoyment from the act of creating and not focus only on the outcome of their work. We need to recognize that creativity cannot be bottled and sold because it works in its own paradoxical ways. We need to embrace and enjoy the creative process itself and allow for the rewards to follow.

So how do we help young children develop their creative potential? Creativity requires changing ways of doing or ways of thinking. It means taking risks and stretching our imaginations to resolve challenges. Creativity is formed as children engage in experiences that focus on process, not a final product. Creativity is found in art, music, and play, but creative thought is also found in science and in confronting daily challenges. Creativity is not about talent, skill, or intelligence. Creativity is not a competition to do something better than others. Creativity is about thinking, exploring, discovering, imagining, combining, and redesigning thoughts and ideas. When children play with loose parts, they combine, redesign, line up, take apart, and put loose parts back together with infinite possibilities. Disposable cups become towers for a castle, wood planks become walkways and bridges to cross over a pretend river, and clothespins can be connected into a tool to get something down from a high shelf. The affordances of loose parts enhance children's creativity and support the development of flexible thinking. Observe young children engaged in designing with tiles. You will notice that they begin by testing different color combinations. As they combine colors to create a variety of compositions, their creativity expands. They gain confidence and mix and match tiles to make complex designs. Their interest is in the process, not the end product. Step back and support them by making more tiles in different colors available. Because no creative process is truly complete until it manifests in a tangible reality, allow children to express their creativity through multiple real experiences in play, art, arguments, discussions, and powerful relationships.

Opportunities and Possibilities to Support Creativity

- Help children redefine a problem and the way they ask questions. Redefining a problem means taking a problem, turning it on its head, and looking at the situation from different and unique angles. This may help children strengthen their analytical skills.
- Support children in thinking outside the box. Give them the time and space to freely explore and be creative. Avoid overscheduling their time.
- Give children the opportunity to make mistakes, come up with multiple questions (even when there is no answer), and allow them to test their hypotheses until they are satisfied. This process is an integral part of creative thinking.
- Encourage children to communicate their ideas and articulate how their concept is different. Children need to be prepared to describe why they think their design has value.
- Expose children to a variety of disciplines, from science and engineering to the arts and humanities. Expose children to diverse knowledge and varied interests to broaden the way they see the world and therefore increase their creativity.
- Start exploring things children know and take them into novel and unknown areas they can investigate. This will keep them engaged and interested in the possibilities of new, exciting discoveries.
- Find joy in the process and not only in the achievement. Avoid focusing on ways of thinking that are easily measured by a standardized test.

CHAPTER 22
Messiness

Creativity is a messy yet sought-after skill. To promote creativity in young children, we need to give them the time and freedom to make messes and freely explore their own capacities. We must give them space to pursue their ideas and passions and the opportunity to make mistakes and solve them. We also need to prepare them for the discomfort of ambiguity. Cultivating a child's creative side may reap long-term rewards, but it also requires relinquishing adult expectations and standardized education. Developing creative thinking is a synergetic process that requires a balance between teaching children how to use tools, materials, and techniques and respecting children's unique creative developmental processes.

As children play with loose parts, they are learning the use of different items and how they connect and work together. Combining the use of real tools, such as hammers and screwdrivers, with wood pieces opens creative thinking possibilities for young children. Creative innovations happen when children engage in inquiry and constantly reframe their questions and theories. This process is not linear, and children need to have an abundance of each item to explore and investigate. Miriam remembers her own daughter needing many wooden blocks to construct complex structures. She would build the tallest and largest towers, knock them down, and start them again. This process seemed meaningless to us. We often wondered why she built only to knock down the structures. As we observed her working, we noticed that each time she knocked down her blocks, she was testing a new solution to the building. Her process was messy yet creative and extraordinary. Today she is a graphic designer working as a creative strategist for a technology-based company.

When I observe the creative process unfolding in young children, I notice that they need to add a lot of paint to a work of art or that they need to have many tiles in a transient art piece. Supporting the development of creativity requires adults to understand the importance of messiness, both in the process of creation and in thinking. We need to embrace the idea that creativity is developed not by answering questions but by generating new questions and reframing old ones. Children need to discover their creative passion and find the media that will allow them to express it. Providing them with the opportunity to explore a variety of loose parts will enable them to analyze and investigate the different creative possibilities the materials have to offer. For example, Diana can be seen creating complex patterns using glass beads combined with beach glass. At one point, she wants to frame her work to explore the size of different spaces. Her father notices her looking at different framed photographs and approaches her to see if she needs any help. Together they find some empty frames and remove the glass. The frame provides Diana with a new space to explore her creativity. Her family knows that she needs large areas to explore, and they have come to understand and work around her large and small installations. They have learned to embrace her creative messiness.

Pinch and Poke

Emma, a child who normally doesn't like to get her hands dirty, found clay to be irresistible. As she freely explored the moist, cool substance, she developed ideas and discovered possibilities. She pulled and pinched the clay. She scraped it with her fingers and pressed her whole hand into it. She poked her index finger into the clay ball and  made a deep hole. Each time she acted on the clay, the clay responded. These transformations captivated, inspired, and empowered Emma to keep experimenting. She used both hands to pull and twist the clay and watched it change shape. She dipped her fingers into water to wash off the clay. When she placed her hands back on the clay, her wet fingers glided over the clay, creating a slippery surface. She ran her fingers along the slick surface and then began to poke sea glass into the clay ball. She dug her fingers into the clay and pinched off pieces as she began to strategize how to cover up all the sea glass. Emma can return to the clay tomorrow, which will encourage sustained inquiry and creativity.

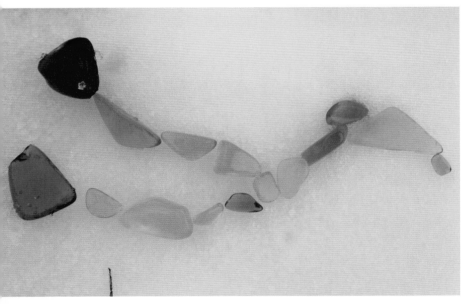

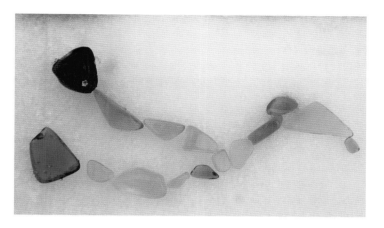

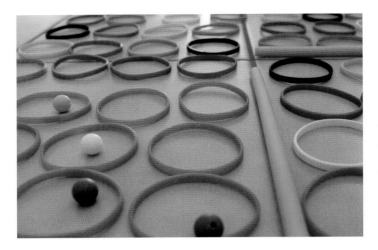

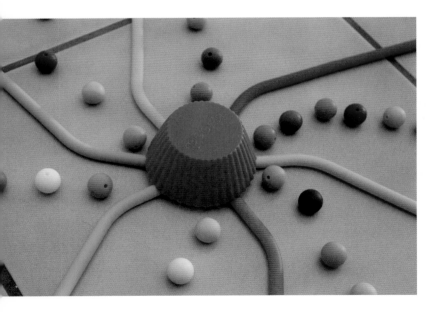

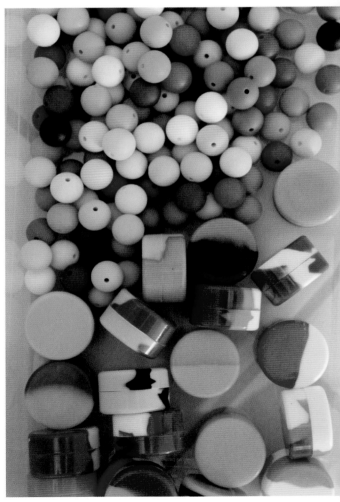

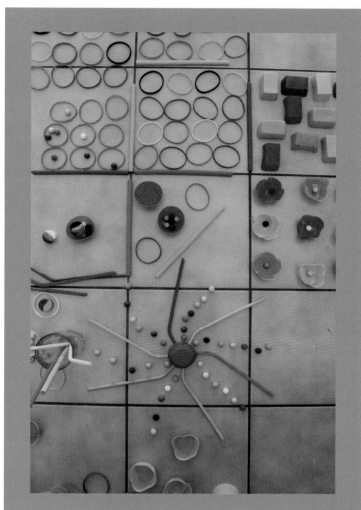

Creativity is messy; children need to add more to their designs before they reach a point of satisfaction. What may seem too much to adults is just the beginning of the process for young children.

CHAPTER 23

Humor and Joy

There is nothing more exciting than listening to a child's laughter. Blissful moments occur when silliness and goofiness take over. We observe a complete abundance of joy. Many inventions, discoveries, solutions, and artistic creations are the result of humor, joy, and giving ourselves permission to have whimsical, silly moments. These are the moments when we fool around with ideas, play with strange possibilities, or turn things upside down, backward, or inside out. When we stretch the limits of our imagination and make room for fun, we enter a state of flow in which our creativity grows, and we are able to innovate, question, and change the rules that constrain our creativity. Humor is an exercise in divergent thinking, an opportunity to see things from a new perspective. Creativity can be sparked when children laugh while a large block structure topples over, when they play with water and large turkey basters, or when they make a catapult and the ball reaches its target.

In Dr. Stuart Brown's (2009, 166) book *Play: How It Shapes the Brain, Opens the Imagination, and Invigorates the Soul*, he promotes humor, identifying it as "the enjoyment of novelty, the capacity to share a lighthearted sense of the world's ironies, the enjoyment of mutual storytelling, the capacity to openly divulge imagination and fantasies." He adds that "when nourished, these playful communications and interactions produce a climate for easy connection and a deepening, more rewarding relationship—true intimacy." Humor and creativity are essential to what makes us human because they reduce stress and allow us to develop empathy and deeper understandings about who we are and the people who surround us. In his book *The Act of Creation*, Arthur Koestler (1964) suggests that humor evokes cognitive, affective, and social processes conducive to creative thinking. Humor seems to connect both brain hemispheres and the frontal lobe, or executive function, of the brain. These connections control major activities such as creativity, relationships, friendship, love, and affection. Laughter and humor create a direct communication link between people. Samuel is a young father who is fully in touch with his own playfulness. He enjoys playing with his children, and their laughter and joy can be felt around the house. They create pirate ships out of crates. Their costumes are designed out of leftover fabric and scarves. They make swords out of rolled newspapers. Their adventures take them to faraway places, where they encounter dragons and find hidden treasures previously hidden by their mother. Their sense of humor can be seen in their dialogue and made-up pirate songs. The role of families in promoting creativity is to rediscover the childlike qualities that allow us to constantly wonder and to embrace the joy and laughter that comes from playing with loose parts.

The Many Colors of the Leaves

During the fall season, as the colors of the leaves change, four-year-old Megan spends time collecting the leaves that have fallen from the trees. She enjoys going on walks and picking up as many leaves as she can. She counts them, sorts them by color and type, and creates transient works of art. If you look at her  designs, you can almost see the ochiba art, the Japanese art of fallen leaves. Her grandfather, who is Japanese, recognizes her work and prints out some of the work by Japanese artists to further inspire her creativity.

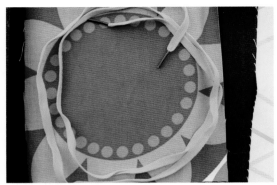

Joy emerges when we discover a new way to solve a problem or combine fabrics to create an innovative work of art.

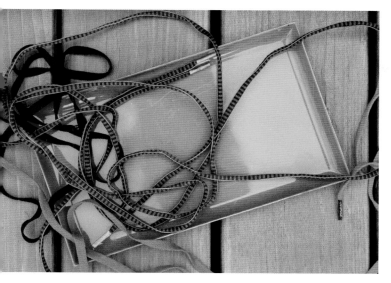

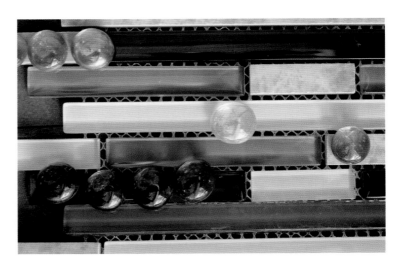

CHAPTER 24

Curiosity and Play

The foundation of creativity is curiosity. Curiosity is the intense need to wonder, discover, and explore new ideas. As children immerse themselves in sustained free play, they draw on their curiosity to ask "what if" and dream of future possibilities. Playfulness encourages children to seek explanations and generate creative hypotheses that lead to new discoveries. The LEGO Foundation conducted a series of studies that demonstrated the important role of play in increasing creativity and promoting cognitive development. Researchers observed that when children play with objects, they are deeply engaged in searching for both personal meaning and an ongoing understanding of themselves in relationship to the environment. Play is a way for children to experiment with the meaning of objects by using their innate curiosity to make sense of the unfamiliar. Children generate creative solutions and innovative products by engaging both curiosity and playfulness, which inspires and motivates others (Ackermann, Gauntlett, and Weckstrom 2009). When children play and explore with objects, ideas, thoughts, or stories from their imagination, they are using their creative capacities to explore a variety of disciplines, from science and technology to creative writing, music, and the visual arts.

Authors Sandra W. Russ and Claire E. Wallace (2013) believe that many cognitive abilities and affective processes important in creativity also occur in pretend play, so pretend play in childhood affects the development of creativity in adulthood. Furthermore, Russ's (2004) research on play identifies fantasy, make-believe, symbolism, organization, cognitive integration of seemingly separate content, and divergent thinking (the ability to come up with many different ideas, story themes, and symbols) as cornerstones of creativity. Renowned psychoanalyst Erik Erikson was quoted as saying, "You see a child play, and it is so close to seeing an artist paint, for in play a child says things without uttering a word. You can see how he solves his problems. You can also see what's wrong. Young children, especially, have enormous creativity, and whatever's in them rises to the surface in free play" (*New York Times* 1994). Erikson creates a link between play and the future creative adult by integrating the following essential core values and traits of a creative person: freedom to express ideas, divergent thinking, problem solving, affective development, flexible thinking, and passion for their work. Sparked by curiosity and sustained by creativity, symbolic play is one of the most joyful things in childhood.

Tiddlywink Caps

For several days, Emma has played with a collection of metal and plastic caps. Each encounter with the materials has resulted in new discoveries. Her curiosity has been visible as she fills and empties bowls, sorts caps, and stacks plastic caps on top of metal caps. She has been captivated with the sound caps make as she stirs them and drops them on the linoleum floor. Today craft sticks are added to the caps. What new possibilities will these materials provide? Emma meticulously lines up seven
metal caps side by side along the area rug's edge. She grasps a craft stick in her right hand and pushes down on a metal cap's edge. To her amazement, the cap flies into the air. She has discovered a new way to play tiddlywinks. She presses cap after cap with the craft stick, watching each one fling into the air and listening to its popping sound. She refines her flicking technique with each press, experimenting with how pressure affects the cap's trajectory. Emma draws on her curiosity as she tests various hypotheses.

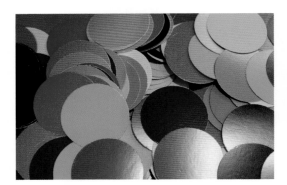

Coasters engage children's creativity as they find pleasure in mixing the different designs to create works of art.

CHAPTER 25

Intellectual and Affective Engagement

Openness to new ideas, experiences, and emotions is critical for both creative and intellectual development. Intellectual engagement is defined by a passion for problem solving, truth seeking, and interacting with new ideas and concepts. On the other hand, affective engagement involves exploring the depths of human emotions and connecting with our instincts, feelings, empathy, and compassion, especially as we make decisions that affect others.

Opportunities for play are steadily declining. Most children are spending the majority of their time in excessively structured activities, which is affecting their overall development. However, in our daily work with loose parts play, we have noticed that children are not only exceeding in all the development domains, but there has also been an increase in symbolic representation and creative thinking. When children play with loose parts, they are experimenting with novel ideas, images, and feelings. They are using their full creative capacity to remain open and curious in their encounters.

The experience of intense emotions is reflected in the work and lives of many famous artists, musicians, and scientists, indicating that emotion may contribute to the creative process. A study led by Dr. Roger Beaty suggests that people with higher levels of creativity show connections between areas of the brain that were not always considered to be linked. The brain is comprised of a series of regions. The default regions are activated when people daydream or engage in wondering and spontaneous thinking. The executive control region, or frontal lobe, of the brain is activated when people need to focus or take control of their own thinking. The salience region of the brain serves as a vehicle that switches between the default and executive areas of the brain. Generally, these regions are activated one at a time, but Beaty discovered that all three are activated at the same time in highly creative people. Additionally, people who are emotionally engaged or open to exploring their emotions seemed to be more open to inspiration, which is a reliable indicator of creativity and intellectual ability (Beaty, Kaufman, and Hyde 2016). When children are given the opportunity to express their genuine emotions and feelings, they are able to engage their creative thinking as they find innovative approaches to make sense of everyday challenges.

Protectors and Guardians

Evelyn is adventurous and experimental. Her art is expansive and imaginative. She spends many happy hours engaged in creative activities that are intricate and innovative. Today she creates an elaborate scene with bottle caps, craft sticks, and dominoes that depicts her understanding of *Harry Potter and the Sorcerer's Stone* and reveals her imaginative capacity. The bottle caps and dominoes at the base of her work are the "protectors and guardians so that bad people can't get in." Craft sticks symbolize the staircase that descends from the trapdoor. As you enter the secret room, there are various bottle caps that have powers: a red cap is the sorcerer's stone, and a blue cap is the "everything stone because it is the most powerful one and can do everything." The colored bottle caps at the very top of Evelyn's scene are fireworks that shoot off like rockets and send messages to different planets. Evelyn may not quite understand the full plot of *Harry Potter and the Sorcerer's Stone*, but her story reveals a common theme of danger and security. Her intellectual and affective engagement help her identify ways to keep bad guys away, warn others, and provide protection.

Lorenzo is fascinated by color. He enjoys exploring a variety of color combinations in his drawings. He is excited when his mother brings home a new cutting board from the Museum of Modern Art. He runs to find his colorful felt balls and spends the rest of the afternoon mixing, matching, and classifying the beautiful colors.

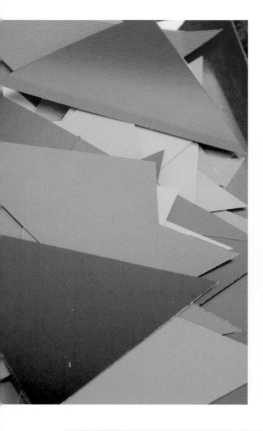

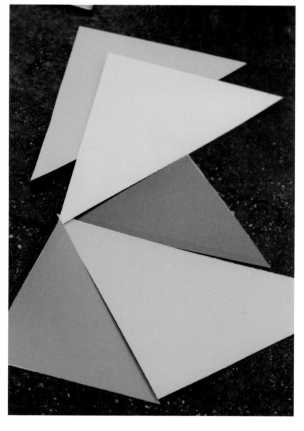

Part 8
Leadership

Open-Mindedness

Altruism

Sustainability

Global Perspective

Now here is my secret. It's quite simple: One sees clearly only with the heart. Anything essential is invisible to the eyes. —ANTOINE DE SAINT-EXUPÉRY, *The Little Prince*

As we look toward the future, we have many questions about what it will take to lead in a world unforeseeable to us. As parents and educators, we recognize that the world is becoming more diverse. We know that children need to build the type of leadership skills that will allow them to communicate and collaborate with many kinds of people. With today's push for academics, children are learning a competitive fill-in-the-bubble mentality that leads them to believe there is only one correct answer to every question. However, future employers want and need people who can think outside the box and solve problems creatively. Success in the workplace also increasingly calls for working cooperatively with diverse teams.

Leadership is required in business, industry, technology, medicine, and the arts all over the world. The role of families and educators becomes critical in assisting with the development of leadership attributes, qualities, and skills. Developing leadership skills helps children build confidence, solve problems creatively, work collaboratively with others, and gain a sense of autonomy and agency within their lives. Even more critical, leadership helps children develop self-concept, which refers to how we perceive ourselves as a physical, social, and moral person. Children's self-esteem shapes their self-concept (how they value their self-worth), self-efficacy (how they assess their ability to perform), and cognitive thought (their knowledge and beliefs). Attributes such as personality, as well as certain physical and mental qualities that support our identity, determine our values and culture, the way we conduct ourselves, and how we relate to other people. The development of these personal attributes is a key contributor to leadership outcomes.

As a parent and educator, Miriam knew that she wanted her daughters to develop leadership skills, but specifically, she wanted them to be altruistic leaders. She wanted them to engage in social-justice work, to speak up against inequity, and to recognize that they have agency in creating a more culturally and environmentally sustainable world. She gave both of her daughters the joy and freedom to play in their early years. Miriam knew that they would have to deal with academics once they entered middle childhood. To create the next generation of leaders who will successfully interact in the global and pluralistic society of the future, we need to provide children with plentiful opportunities to engage in open-ended play. If you have any doubts regarding how play helps develop leadership skills, observe a group of children involved in superhero play. Superheroes are natural leaders, courageous, and powerful, and they overcome incredible obstacles with patience, responsibility, and empathy.

Superhero play also instills a strong sense of social justice through building the capacities to listen, empathize, and understand alternative perspectives. Leadership skills are necessary for children to be successful in their future endeavors and essential to gaining an altruistic and open-minded view of the world that will lead them to create a sustainable future.

Opportunities and Possibilities to Support Leadership

- Provide loose parts that promote symbolic play and opportunities for role play.
- Engage children in authentic conversations about empathy and compassion. Listen to the play and find moments to enter the discussion.
- Reflect on your ideas, interests, feelings, and opinions and how they affect the way you interact with children. Take the time to play with loose parts.
- Focus on perseverance and on process, not perfection. Create opportunities to make mistakes and to change the outcome. Loose parts are open ended, thus allowing children to value the process instead of the final product.
- Build negotiation skills and know that arguments are not harmful; they are a way for children to express their ideas and feelings. Guide children to have powerful conversations. When children play with loose parts, they engage in arguments, collaboration, and problem solving.
- Trust children's capacities and support them when they have an idea. There is no right or wrong thinking when children play with loose parts; instead there is a world of thinking possibilities.
- Help children build agency through altruism and social-justice work. They will learn that they can make a meaningful change.
- Recycle and upcycle loose parts to contribute to a sustainable environment.

CHAPTER 26

Open-Mindedness and Perspective-Taking

The ability to get along with others and develop authentic connections with peers and adults will help children work more effectively in the future. Open-mindedness, the willingness to try new things or hear and consider new ideas, is essential in the successful formation and development of relationships with others. An open mind is anchored in the desire to find truth and understanding. Open-mindedness is listening flexibly and fairly to competing perspectives and learning from other points of view. Closely related is the capacity of perspective-taking, perceiving a situation or understanding a concept from an alternative point of view. Perspective-taking begins when children can identify, name, and understand different emotions both in themselves and others. Perspective-taking, however, is not the same thing as empathy. Being able to identify and feel sadness with another person is essential in human relationships, but it is not the same as understanding what sadness might feel like to that person, or why the sadness exists. We must consider empathy as separate from, but still an integral part of, both perspective-taking and open-mindedness. To engage in collaborative work, children need to gain the capacity for perspective-taking and be open-minded about differences between people. These capacities are connected and support each other to help children acquire the skills to build friendships and work in collaborative environments with other people.

Perspective-taking and open-mindedness are central elements to be a leader. In her book *Mind in the Making: The Seven Essential Life Skills Every Child Needs*, Ellen Galinsky, author and president of the Families and Work Institute, discusses perspective-taking as developing from specific childhood capacities, including cognitive flexibility and symbolic play.

Cognitive Flexibility

Cognitive flexibility is the ability to switch our attention from one situation to another, adjust to change, and accommodate for new and innovative ideas, even if they differ from our own. This capacity is critical as children become adults and enter the workforce; they must be able to shift their focus from one project or idea and refocus their attention on a different project or creative solution. The ability to successfully multitask and adapt to change using cognitive flexibility will be essential to future leaders.

Symbolic Play

Symbolic play is crucial for children to develop perspective-taking and open-mindedness. In symbolic play, they take on different roles that help them understand how people may feel and think. Yoli uses string and buttons to create a stethoscope. She brings it to her doll's heart and says, "I am the doctor, and I will take care of you because I see that you are hurting." In symbolic play, children often construct their understanding of how the world works. They not only use their own experiences, but they also incorporate their imagination and creativity. Consider creating small worlds, which are miniature imaginative play scenes. You can create small worlds using containers, trays, planters, boxes, or wine barrels. Small worlds usually have natural sensory components, such as sand, dirt, gravel, or pebbles. Include loose parts to increase the play possibilities. For example, shells and sand can inspire children to explore the ocean. Gravel and small blocks can help children re-create a construction site. Listen to the children and take note of their interests to give you more ideas of what you can add to the small-world play. Small-world play promotes social interactions and opportunities to connect with other children while also giving children the chance to play alone and reflect on challenges they may be experiencing. In play children make sense of the world and deepen their understanding of what other people think, feel, and understand. Through this type of symbolic play, children begin to gain a deeper understanding of their responsibilities and their roles as leaders.

Building a Town

Tayron and Chantell have been noticing that their neighborhood is changing, and more tall buildings have been built. They are concerned about where they will play if more buildings take over their park. They re-create their neighborhood using small blocks and wooden half rings, moving the blocks in different ways to consider how to protect their park. In the afternoon, their neighbor Shawn joins them in the planning. They discuss how they can bring their ideas to the people that build the buildings. Tayron and Chantell's mother encourages them to take a photo of the plans and to write a letter to the builders. The next day, they take the letter and the photo and deliver it to the foreman of the project. In this simple act, the three children have been open to a new idea and have learned that they can take a leadership role in making changes in their community.

This series of photos reveals how children used perspective-taking to consider how a different group of people might perceive landing in snow. Creatures from outer space have landed on a new planet with a terrain that is foreign to them. The creatures are challenged to create a base station in the unusual cold, white substance and go about building protection towers, transmitters, and receivers.

CHAPTER 27

Altruism and Social Justice

For many families, social justice is a challenging topic. The instinct may be to shield children from what we consider to be politically, socially, and economically charged discourse. However, social justice is about so much more than the topics we might consider to be harmful; social justice includes fairness, equality, acceptance, diversity, trust, and kindness. If you listen to the conversation in a superhero play scenario, you see that children are already developing a sense of what is "fair" and what is "not fair." They are critical thinkers and notice that there are groups of people in the world who are treated better than others, especially when the media is loaded with these types of messages. Therefore starting social justice work with our youngest citizens is crucial. Children are in the process of making sense of how the world functions, and they are learning through social interactions and the environments and communities in which they live.

In their work on anti-bias education (ABE), authors Louise Derman-Sparks and Julie Olsen Edwards advise us that young children need the guidance and support of caring adults to help them construct positive messages about themselves and others. Children need guidance to learn to navigate and resist the harmful impact of prejudice and discrimination. Laying the foundation for social-justice work must start in early childhood and continue throughout children's lifespans. With appropriate adult guidance, this foundation can be built upon and provide children the leadership skills they need to function in a diverse world (Derman-Sparks and Olsen Edwards 2015).

Building a Hospital

When Maya's younger brother is hospitalized, to bring a sense of normalcy to Maya, her grandmother invites the neighborhood children to play in Maya's apartment. Maya's family does not have a lot of money, but they are creative in the play items they provide the children. Maya's father works in a printing shop, so he saves tubes from different printing

jobs. The tubes serve as blocks for building. Maya and her friends spend afternoons building the hospital where her brother is staying. The children take turns playing doctors, nurses, and other patients. The recurring theme is one of gender. Matthew and Jamal want to be the doctors because they are boys. They tell Maya and Frances to be nurses because girls

cannot be doctors. Their building continues, along with the conversations. Finally Maya's grandmother intervenes and helps the children understand that both boys and girls can be doctors and nurses. More importantly she takes the time to listen to the children's perspectives and experiences. She asks open-ended questions: "Who makes decisions, and who is left out?" "Who is enjoying the play, and who is not?" "Why are only boys doctors, and only girls nurses, and is that fair or unfair?" and "How can we change the play so that both boys and girls can be doctors and nurses?" These questions help the children understand how using power to prevent other children from assuming specific roles is not fair or helpful to other people.

Ariana and Sofia have been spending their days building enclosures and tall walls of cardboard tubes and then knocking them over. When their mom inquires about why they are knocking over their structures, they state that they are "bashing down walls that keep people out." Once their mom realizes that her daughters are processing recent political events, they are able to have a conversation about the impact of a border wall on families in the United States and Mexico.

CHAPTER 28
Building Sustainability

Living sustainably means living within the capacity of our natural environment and ensuring that our actions have minimal negative impact on the world around us, including our society and culture. Sustainability considers everything from pollution, industrialism, and recycling to consumerism, commercialism, and community well-being.

Concern about children's access to the outside world continues to grow. As opportunities for outdoor play diminish, children are becoming disconnected from nature, which prevents them from gaining the foundational principle to respect and sustain the environment for future generations. When children are outside, they are often conscious of what is happening to the environment. They notice when there is trash in the park or when the river water is murky from pollutants. They may hear about the importance of sustaining the environment from family or the media. Children have the capacity and inclination to both advocate and care for their environment. Teaching them about sustainability helps them become active citizens within their communities and advances the world toward a more sustainable society. Because young children are concrete thinkers, understanding sustainability needs to be rooted in their daily reality to demonstrate the direct impact of sustainability on their lives. As children collect and play with upcycled materials such as bottle caps, engage them in a conversation about how saving the caps and using them in their play is contributing to the well-being of environment. Go on walks and collect pine cones, acorns, liquid amber, and oak balls. Save them and have the children share them with others. Talk with them about how these beautiful gifts of nature exist only when we all contribute to sustaining the environment. As children engage in understanding their role in creating a sustainable future, they will know that their actions support the actions of other children around the world. Fundamental values, attitudes, skills, habits, and behaviors begin to form in early childhood and tend to be long lasting. Children develop a sense of agency and leadership when they participate in sustainability efforts. They feel, see, and understand that their ideas and opinions are valued. They know that they are capable of making sustainable change and contributing to the betterment of their community. These are important values and attitudes that serve as the foundation for becoming a conscious and sustainable adult.

Making Perfume

David, Daniel, and Anna have been collecting small glass and plastic bottles. They want to make perfume and sell it to raise money to help the local homeless shelter. When they finally have enough bottles, they spend time with their dad reading recipes for making perfume. They decide that grinding flowers and spices and mixing them with water and oils is the best idea. They experiment with different flowers,  from roses in their garden to gardenias from their grandmother's house. They grind mint and rosemary from their mom's herb garden and add a few drops of oil. They test the perfume and have their mom, aunt, and grandma try it. They all agree that the perfume has a nice smell and is ready to be bottled. The children carefully fill the bottles using small funnels. They add labels with their drawings and argue about how much they will charge. The next day, they set up a small table outside their house and offer the bottles of perfume to the neighbors. At the end of the day, they count the money and are excited that they made ten dollars to donate to the shelter. It was hard work, but their commitment to help the people in the shelter kept them focused. They have learned to take leadership and give back to the community they live in and have participated in sustaining the environment by recycling the small perfume bottles and making money for the local homeless shelter.

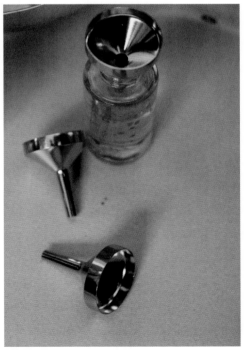

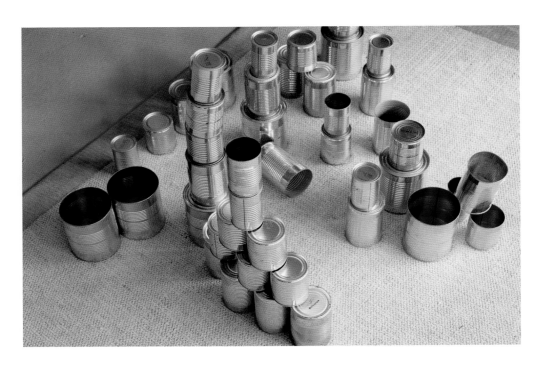

Upcycling is free and resourceful. Repurposing aluminum cans into building materials is a great form of upcycling and a way to reduce unnecessary waste. Their uniformity in shape and size makes cans perfect for building, stacking, and nesting,

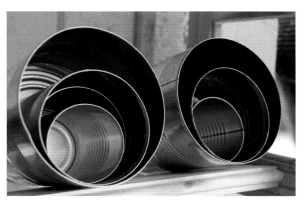

CHAPTER 29

A Global Perspective

A core value in many families and early childhood programs is raising children to care about their community, society, and world that they live in. At an early age, we are telling children that they need to share. We want to instill the capacity for altruism and empathy. We want children to work collaboratively and engage in teamwork. We also want children to think critically and make decisions that are based on facts, knowledge, and thoughtful reflection so that they can make empathic connections to the ideas and perspectives of people different than themselves.

Teaching children to be caring citizens of the world grows from their emergent concerns. Because of the open-ended qualities of loose parts, children can negotiate, hypothesize, think critically, make connections, notice differences and similarities, compromise, and come up with creative and innovative solutions to complex issues. Listen to their conversations and discourse and observe the themes that emerge in their play. Children are filled with concerns about their identity, giving to others, fairness, and relationships. Children have an instinctive capacity to make sense of their social and cultural world. When adults join them in their pursuit for answers, they help children's thinking become rooted in accurate and empathic understandings. Leaving them to make their conclusions might lead to misinformation, cultural bias, and stereotypical thinking. When children play, they enter a zone of more profound reflection, and they make sense of what is happening in their lives. When adults take the opportunity to engage with children in questions about identity and equity, we participate in the work of reshaping our society.

Once children gain knowledge of how different people participate in the world, understand different perspectives, and develop empathy for others, they can begin to take action that makes a change in their community. Social justice, altruism, and sustainability cannot be taught in one easy lesson; they are values that need to be integrated into every aspect of a child's life. By making children feel safe and guiding them to these values, families can help their children ask the right questions and participate in ways that are purposeful and productive. These are all essential skills needed to live in a global society, and play with loose parts is the perfect vehicle for developing them.

Discovering the World

Natalia and Mariana discover their great-grandmother's stamp collection. They enjoy looking at the stamps through a magnifying glass and noticing all the details. They look at the envelopes and wonder where the letters came from. They set up a small office space and pretend to write letters to send to children in other countries. Their great-grandma sits down with them and shares the stories of the stamps she remembers. She shares that some of the stamps came from letters sent to her by her sister living in Venezuela. Natalia and Mariana continue to sort and classify the stamps. They arrange them in beautiful and intricate designs. In this simple play, they are learning about the world and making connections to what it means to be a global citizen.

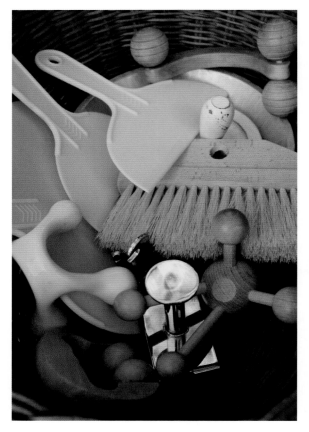

As children play in the dirt and garden, they can learn how important dirt is to human well-being and security for growing food.

At the heart of children's lives everywhere is the right to play (United Nations General Assembly 1989). We have a responsibility to protect this right on behalf of our own children and children around the world.

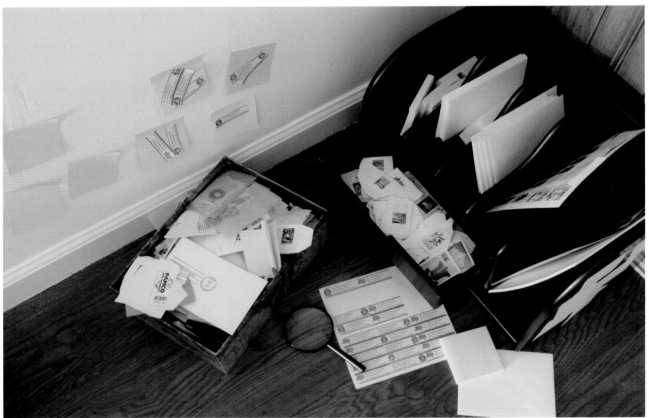

References

Ackermann, Edith, David Gauntlett, and Cecilia Weckstrom. 2009. *Defining Systematic Creativity*. The LEGO Foundation. http://davidgauntlett.com/wp-content /uploads/2013/05/LEGO_LLI09_Systematic_Creativity_PUBLIC.pdf.

American Academy of Pediatrics. 2016. "Policy Statement: Media and Young Minds." *Pediatrics* 138 (5): e20162591.

Beaty, Roger, Scott B. Kaufman, and Elizabeth Hyde. 2016. *Toward an Imagination Science: Neuroscience Imagination Retreat*. Report prepared by Department of Psychology and Center for Brain Science, Harvard University. Philadelphia: Imagination Institute. December 2–4.

Beghetto, Ronald A. 2009. "Correlates of Intellectual Risk Taking in Elementary School Science." *Journal of Research in Science Teaching* 46 (2): 210–23. https://doi .org/10.1002/tea.20270.

Brown, Brené. 2012. *Daring Greatly: How the Courage to Be Vulnerable Transforms the Way We Live, Love, Parent, and Lead*. New York: Gotham Books.

Brown, Stuart. 2009. *Play: How It Shapes the Brain, Opens the Imagination, and Invigorates the Soul*. New York: Avery.

Bruner, Jerome. 1996. *The Culture of Education*. Cambridge, MA: Harvard University Press.

Carson, Rachel. 1998. *The Sense of Wonder*. New York: HarperCollins.

Christakis, Erika. 2016a. *The Importance of Being Little: What Young Children Really Need from Grownups*. New York: Viking.

———. 2016b. "The New Preschool Is Crushing Kids." *The Atlantic*, January/February.

Clements, Douglas H., and Michelle Stephan. 2003. "Measurement in Pre-K to Grade 2 Mathematics." In *Engaging Young Children in Mathematics: Standards for Early Childhood Mathematics Education*, edited by Douglas. H. Clements, Julie Sarama, and Ann-Marie DiBiase, 299–318. Mahwah, NJ: Lawrence Erlbaum Associates.

Coles, Robert. 1997. *The Moral Intelligence of Children*. New York: Random House.

Csikszentmihalyi, Mihaly. 1997. *Finding Flow: The Psychology of Engagement with Everyday Life*. New York: Basic Books. Kindle.

———. 2013. *Creativity: Flow and the Psychology of Discovery and Invention*. New York: Harper Perennial.

DeBenedet, Anthony T., and Lawrence Cohen. 2010. *The Art of Roughhousing: Good Old-Fashioned Horseplay and Why Every Kid Needs It*. Philadelphia: Quirk Books. Kindle.

Derman-Sparks, Louise, and Julie Olsen Edwards. 2015. "Teaching Young Children about Race: A Guide for Parents and Teachers." Teaching for Change. www.teachingforchange.org/teaching-about-race.

DeVries, Rheta, and Betty Zan. 2012. *Moral Classrooms, Moral Children: Creating a Constructivist Atmosphere in Early Education*. New York: Teachers College Press.

Dewey, John. 1916. *Democracy and Education. An Introduction to the Philosophy of Education*. New York: The Macmillan Company.

Elkind, David. 1988. *The Hurried Child: Growing Up Too Fast Too Soon*. Reading, MA: Addison Wesley.

———. 2008. "The Power of Play: Learning What Comes Naturally." *American Journal of Play* 1 (1): 1–6.

Galinsky, Ellen. 2010. *Mind in the Making: The Seven Essential Life Skills Every Child Needs*. New York: HarperCollins.

Gibson, James J. 1979. *The Ecological Approach to Visual Perception*. Boston: Houghton Mifflin.

Gill, Tim. 2007. *No Fear: Growing Up in a Risk Averse Society*. London: Calouste Gulbenkian Foundation.

Ginsburg, Kenneth, the Committee on Communications, and the Committee on Psychosocial Aspects of Child and Family Health. 2007. "The Importance of Play in Promoting Healthy Child Development and Maintaining Strong Parent-Child Bonds." *Pediatrics* 119, no. 1 (January): 182–91.

Gopnik, Alison, David M. Sobel, Laura E. Schulz, and Clark Glymour. 2001. "Causal Learning Mechanisms in Very Young Children: Two-, Three-, and Four-Year-Olds Infer Causal Relations from Patterns of Variation and Covariation." *Developmental Psychology* 37 (5): 620–29. https://doi.org/10.1037//0012-1649.37.5.620.

Gray, Peter. 2013. *Free to Learn: Why Unleashing the Instinct to Play Will Make Our Children Happier, More Self-Reliant, and Better Students for Life*. New York: Basic Books.

Herrington, Susan, Chandra Lesmeister, Jamie Nicholls, and Kate Stefiuk. 2007. *7Cs: An Informational Guide to Young Children's Outdoor Play Spaces*. Vancouver, BC: Consortium for Health, Intervention, Learning and Development (CHILD). https://sala.ubc.ca/sites/sala.ubc.ca/files/documents/7Cs.pdf.

Herron, R. E., and Brian Sutton-Smith. 1971. *Child's Play*. New York: Wiley.

Institute of Medicine. 2000. *From Neurons to Neighborhoods: The Science of Early Childhood Development*. Washington, DC: The National Academies Press. https://doi.org/10.17226/9824.

International Play Association. 2008. *IPA Declaration of the Child's Right to Play*. http://ipaworld.org/childs-right-to-play/the-childs-right-to-play.

Jablon, Judy R., and Michael Wilkinson. 2006. "Using Engagement Strategies to Facilitate Children's Learning and Success." *Young Children* 61 (2): 12–16.

Jung, Rex E. 2014. "Evolution, Creativity, Intelligence, and Madness: 'Here Be Dragons.'" *Frontiers in Psychology*. https://doi.org/10.3389/fpsyg.2014.00784.

Kaufman, Scott Barry, and Carolyn Gregoire. 2015. *Wired to Create: Unraveling the Mysteries of the Creative Mind*. New York: Penguin. Kindle.

Keene, Ellin Oliver. 2018. *Engaging Children: Igniting a Drive for Deeper Learning K–8*. Portsmouth, NH: Heinemann.

Kerr, Barbara, ed. 2009. *Encyclopedia of Giftedness, Creativity and Talent*. Vol. 2. Thousand Oaks, CA: Sage Publications.

Koestler, Arthur. 1964. *The Act of Creation*. New York: Macmillan.

Marulis, Loren M., and Susan B. Neuman. 2010. "The Effects of Vocabulary Intervention on Young Children's Word Learning: A Meta-Analysis." *Review of Educational Research* 80 (3): 300–335. https://steinhardt.nyu.edu/scmsAdmin/media/users/sn1150 /marulisNeuman.pdf.

Maslow, Abraham H. 1987. *Motivation and Personality*. 3rd ed. New York: Harper & Row.

Miller, Edward, and Joan Almon. 2009. "Crisis in the Kindergarten: Why Children Need to Play in School." College Park, MD: Alliance for Childhood.

National Institute for Literacy. 2009. *Early Beginnings: Early Literacy Knowledge and Instruction. A Guide for Early Childhood Administrators and Professional Development Providers*. https://lincs.ed.gov/publications/pdf/NELPEarlyBeginnings09.pdf.

Nicholson, Simon. 1971. "How NOT to Cheat Children: The Theory of Loose Parts." *Landscape Architecture* 62:30–34.

New York Times. 1994. Obituary for Erik Erikson. *New York Times*, May 13, C16. https:// www.nytimes.com/1994/05/13/obituaries/erik-erikson-91-psychoanalyst-who -reshaped-views-of-human-growth-dies.html.

OECD (Organization for Economic Co-operation and Development) and CERI (Centre for Educational Research and Innovation). 2008. *21st Century Learning: Research, Innovation and Policy: Directions from Recent OECD Analyses*. http://www.oecd.org/site /educeri21st/40554299.pdf.

Oswalt, Angela. 2019. "Early Childhood Emotional and Social Development: Identity and Self-Esteem. Child Development and Parenting." PermiaCare. Accessed June 25. pbmhmr.com/poc/view_doc.php?type=doc&id=12766&cn=462.

Panksepp, Jaak. 2014. *Affective Neuroscience: The Foundations of Human and Animal Emotions*. Oxford: Oxford University Press.

Partnership for 21st Century Learning. 2019. "Framework for 21st Century Learning Definitions." Battelle for Kids. http://static.battelleforkids.org/documents/p21/P21 _Framework_DefinitionsBFK.pdf.

Pellis, Sergio M., Vivien C. Pellis, and Heather C. Bell. 2010. "The Function of Play in the Development of the Social Brain." *American Journal of Play* 2 (3): 278–96.

Pelo, Ann. 2009. "A Pedagogy for Ecology." *Rethinking Schools* 23, no. 4 (Summer). www.rethinkingschools.org/articles/a-pedagogy-for-ecology.

Perry, Bruce D. 2016. "Emotional Development: Creating an Emotionally Safe Classroom." *Early Childhood Today.* www.scholastic.com/teachers/articles /teaching-content/emotional-development-creating-emotionally-safe-classroom/.

Pistorova, Stacey, and Ruslan Slutsky. 2017. "There Is Still Nothing Better Than Quality Play Experiences for Young Children's Learning and Development: Building the Foundation for Inquiry in Our Educational Practices." *Early Child Development and Care* 188 (5): 495–507. https://doi.org/10.1080/03004430.2017.1403432.

Portis, Antoinette. 2006. *Not a Box.* New York: HarperCollins.

Robinson, Ken. 2017. *Out of Our Minds: Learning to Be Creative.* Chichester, West Sussex: John Wiley and Son. Kindle.

Rogers, Carl R. 1954. "Toward a Theory of Creativity." *ETC: A Review of General Semantics* 11, no. 4: 249–60. www.jstor.org/stable/42581167.

Rogers, Fred. 2003. *The World according to Mister Rogers: Important Things to Remember.* New York: Hyperion.

Russ, Sandra W. 2004. *Play in Child Development and Psychotherapy: Toward Empirically Supported Practice.* Mahwah, NJ: Lawrence Erlbaum Associates.

Russ, Sandra W., and Claire E. Wallace. 2013. "Pretend Play and Creative Processes." *American Journal of Play* 6 (1): 136–48.

Saint-Exupéry, Antoine de. 2000. *The Little Prince.* Orlando, FL: Harcourt.

Schulz, Amy, and Rajinder Gill. 2014. *Community Colleges and 21st Century Skills: Skills Panels to Assist Student Career Success.* New World of Work. https://www .newworldofwork.org/wp-content/uploads/2016/10/New-World-of-Work-Skills -Panel-Report-April-2014.pdf.

ten Boom, Corrie. 1971. *The Hiding Place.* New York: Bantam.

Tyagi, Vaibhav, Yaniv Hanoch, Stephen D. Hall, Mark Runco, and Susan L. Denham. 2017. "The Risky Side of Creativity: Domain Specific Risk Taking in Creative Individuals." *Frontiers in Psychology* 8:145. www.doi.org/10.3389/fpsyg.2017.00145.

United Nations Committee on the Rights of the Child. 2013. "General Comment No. 17 on the Right of the Child to Rest, Leisure, Play, Recreational Activities, Cultural Life and the Arts." https://www.refworld.org/docid/51ef9bcc4.html.

United Nations General Assembly. 1989. *Convention on the Rights of the Child.* United Nations, Treaty Series 1577 (November 20): 3. www.refworld.org/docid/3ae6b38f0. html.

Van Hoorn, Judith, Patricia Monighan Nourot, Barbara Scales, and Keith Rodriguez Alward. 2007. *Play at the Center of Curriculum.* 4th ed. Upper Saddle River, NJ: Pearson Prentice Hall.

Wagner, Tony. 2012. *Creating Innovators: The Making of Young People Who Will Change the World.* New York: Scribner.

Weller, Chris. 2018. "Silicon Valley Parents Are Raising Their Kids Tech-Free—and It Should Be a Red Flag." *Business Insider*, February 2018. www.businessinsider.com /silicon-valley-parents-raising-their-kids-tech-free-red-flag-2018-2.

Wilson, Edward O. 2017. *The Origins of Creativity*. New York: Liveright. Kindle.

Woodland Tribe. 2018. Accessed July 2. www.woodlandtribe.org.

World Economic Forum. 2016. *The Future of Jobs: Employment, Skills, and Workforce Strategy for the Fourth Industrial Revolution.* www3.weforum.org/docs/WEF _Future_of_Jobs.pdf.

Yale Poorvu Center for Teaching and Learning. 2018. "Bloom's Taxonomy." Accessed September 12. https://ctl.yale.edu/BloomsTaxonomy.

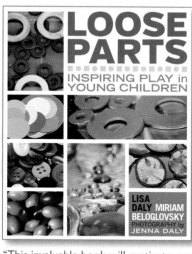
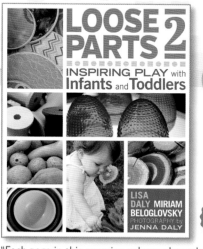